MathArts

2nd EDITION

Other Books by MaryAnn F. Kohl

Action Art with Barbara Zaborowski

Discovering Great Artists with Kim Solga

Good Earth Art with Cindy Gainer

Great American Artists for Kids with Kim Solga

Making Make-Believe

Mudworks

Mudworks, Bilingual Edition

Science Arts with Jean Potter

Scribble Art

Storybook Art with Jean Potter

MathArts

2nd EDITION

EXPLORING MATH THROUGH ART FOR 3 TO 6 YEAR OLDS

MaryAnn F. Kohl & **Cindy Gainer**

CHICAGO REVIEW PRESS

Dedication

To the memory of my parents, J.R. and Betty Faubion, who gave me love and room to grow, time to play, and lots of books and art supplies. —MAK

MathArts is dedicated with love to my husband Bill, who helps me to keep things in perspective, and to my son August who gives me joy and reminds me daily of childhood. —CG

Copyright © 2019 by MaryAnn F. Kohl and Cindy Gainer
All rights reserved
First edition published in 1996 by Gryphon House, Inc.

Published by Chicago Review Press, Incorporated
814 North Franklin Street
Chicago, Illinois 60610
ISBN 978-1-64160-024-8

Library of Congress Cataloging-in-Publication Data is available from the Library of Congress.

Cover design: Andrew Brozyna
Cover photos, left to right on front: Shutterstock, Andrew Brozyna; back, iStockphoto
Interior illustrations: Cindy Gainer

Printed in the United States of America
5 4 3 2 1

Dear Reader

When we first thought about the intriguing idea of young children learning math through art, we looked at the world of young children and found that they are constantly exposed to math and art as an integrated, natural part of each day. For example, they:

- ✓ notice a pattern of colors in a string of beads
- ✓ see a juicy, ripe apple cut in half for a snack that becomes two equal divided halves, with identical designs on each half
- ✓ mix two cups of flour and two cups of salt to make a playdough recipe
- ✓ build a sculpture with blocks and then sort the blocks into piles that are similar in some way, such as one pile for building walls, one pile for roofs and one pile for fences
- ✓ play with a heavy rock and a light pebble
- ✓ press muddy fingertips on a T-shirt creating a print or pattern
- ✓ notice the patterns of polka dots on a favorite shirt.

MathArts is a collection of easy, creative art experiences integrated with early math concepts, activities that increase the young child's awareness of math through art. With the activities in *MathArts* young children can explore math concepts from their everyday world, such as

- ✓ matching and sorting
- ✓ patterns, sequence, and order
- ✓ one-to-one correspondence
- ✓ spatial relationships such as direction, boundaries, and the whole and its parts
- ✓ number values and recognizing numerals
- ✓ counting and measuring

Using paint, paper, dough, twigs, glue, and blocks and many other easy-to-find materials, the young child explores math concepts in developmentally appropriate learning experiences.

One thing we discovered when writing, testing, and developing the ideas in this book is that children LOVE mathart projects! They are familiar and comfortable with art, live math every day at home and at school or child care, and really enjoy doing process art experiences that bring the two together. And, adults like mathart, too.

Let's start counting, cutting, and creating! The children are way ahead of us!

Sincerely,
MaryAnn Kohl and Cindy Gainer

Using the Icons

Each activity has up to four icons to make the projects in *MathArts* more useable and accessible. These icons are suggestions, subject to your personal and individual modifications or changes based on your experience and needs. Experiment with materials, vary suggested techniques, or modify projects to suit the needs and abilities of each artist or each adult. Creative variation is part of the fun of providing mathart experiences.

Age

  Age indicates the general age range where a child can create and explore independently, that is, without much adult assistance. The "+" means that children this age and all ages older should be comfortable doing the project. However, children younger than the suggested age can also do the project with adult assistance. Children do not always fit the standard developmental expectations of a particular age, so decide which projects suit individual children and their specific abilities and needs.

Planning or Preparation

Easy   Moderate   Involved

This icon indicates the degree of planning or preparation time an adult will need to collect materials, set up the activity, or supervise the activity. Icons shown indicate planning and preparation time that is easy, moderate, or involved.

Help

 The help icon indicates the artist may need extra assistance from another child or from an adult during this activity.

Caution

 The icon appears for all activities that suggest the use of sharp, hot, or electrical materials. All activities require supervision, but activities with the caution icon need extra care.

Table of Contents

Part I: I've Just Begun...Exploring Counting

Chapter 1: Almost Counting, One Is One

One-to-One Correspondence

Measuring Materials

Counting

Shape Recognition

Matching

Chapter 2: Many Kinds of Many Kinds

Sorting and Classifying

Chapter 3: One, Two, Red, Blue

Patterns

Sequence

Order

Part 2: I'm on My Way...Exploring Spatial Relationships

Chapter 4: Near, Far, Up, Down

Chapter 5: Fences, Frames, Boxes

Chapter 6: Parts and Pieces

Part 3: Look at Me Go...Exploring Number Value

Chapter 7: Really Counting

Chapter 8: How Many Is Many?

Acknowledgments

Cindy, my coauthor, for her motivation and friendship.

All the young artists in Bellingham, Washington, for the ideas they have given me and for showing me how to improve the ideas I already have.

My daughters, Hannah and Megan, for their praise and encouragement.

Michael, for his great ideas and for enjoying what I do as much as I do.

— MAK

MaryAnn, my coauthor, for her talent and expertise.

Karen Cameron Scanlon, EdD, whose knowledge of mathematics for the young child has been a great resource to me.

Jack Irwin for his technical assistance.

Special thanks to William A. Sorrels, MEd, who taught me the concept of the whole and inspired me to write activities for *MathArts* that assist children in whole development.

— CG

Introduction

Math is part of everyday life—noticing the shape of blocks, setting the table with the correct number of places, measuring ingredients for a recipe, remembering what comes next in a story. *MathArts* uses everyday experiences and materials to explore the concepts of math through hands-on art activities. Children learn actively, building a foundation for more complex math skills. The activities in this book contain a wealth of easy-to-do, creative art experiences that encourage children's natural development of math concepts.

Examples of mathart explorations are:

patterns—stringing handmade clay beads on a necklace

shapes—creating a crayon rubbing of cardboard shapes

matching—painting a shapes mural using the overhead projector

sorting—creating a paper scrap collage by colors

order—gluing the smallest to the largest wood blocks in a sculpture

sequence—a photography display of events

spatial relationships—creating a mobile with wood curls

direction—painting left and right sides of the face

symmetry—making prints with bubbles

boundaries—crafting a papier-mâché frame for an original artwork

separation and division—pressing pieces of clay together in a relief

counting—creating original, baked clay counters and buttons

number value—hiding cotton balls in a number sculpture

making numerals—sculpting bread dough number shapes

graphing—comparing favorite colors of children's original paintings in a collage

measuring—mixing a paint dough recipe

weighing—creating a hanging mobile scale

time—timing silly squiggle drawings

money—creating original clay coins

The development of math skills and understanding is unique to each child and need not be forced. Providing a wealth of materials and hands-on explorations and experiences allows the young child to progress in his own way, in his own time. Exploring and discovering helps the child understand math concepts more completely. Many of the projects in *MathArts* repeat concepts over and over using new materials and techniques to give the early learner a chance to rediscover and refine concepts and skills while developing new ones.

In MathArts...

✓ the learner is an active participant in the learning and creating process.

✓ math is presented through inviting, easily managed art ideas that allow the child to discover concepts independently.

✓ math and art are integrated to link the two areas as one.

✓ understanding early math concepts occurs through creative art experiences that stress process, not product.

✓ children are encouraged to explore, discover, and create.

In MathArts the child...

✓ manipulates concrete materials through art media.

✓ creates with available objects and common art materials.

✓ discovers math concepts through exploration and creative art experiences.

✓ works as an individual, as a partner, in small groups, and in large groups.

✓ explores and discovers through the process of art rather than focusing on the finished product.

✓ extends and refines ideas by repeating math concepts with new art ideas, materials, and experiences.

✓ makes decisions on how to progress through a project based on individual needs, previous learning, and unique experiences.

MathArts uses materials commonly found in the home or classroom and materials that can be easily collected from free resources. To make "reuse, recycle, and recreate" work we must all have a bit of the scavenger in our hearts and souls. When you get really good at it, your collection of supplies will grow into a treasure trove. Several materials that are used in *MathArts* projects have sources that are free for the asking, such as these commonly used materials:

Matte Board—available from frame shops in a variety of sizes, shapes, colors, and textures. Bring a box and ask the frame shop if they will save scraps for you. Sometimes they will let you go through their scrap pile and select your own. Matte board scraps and frame shapes are a common material in this book.

Paper—available from quality printing shops in a variety of colors, textures, and sizes. Some scraps are shredded, others are still in beautiful full sheets. They come in poster size and confetti size. Bring a box and ask the shop to save paper for you. They may allow you to go through their scrap pile and select your own. Other types of paper include construction paper, photocopy paper, and butcher paper.

Cardboard Tubes—ask people (parents, friends, family) to save their paper towel and toilet paper tubes for your mathart projects.

Boxes—available in many sizes and shapes from hosiery, jewelry, gifts, foods, and shipping cartons. Ask other people to save them for you. Ask departments stores to save hosiery, jewelry, and gift folders for you. Shoe stores may save shoe and boot boxes. Bring a large carton or plastic garbage bag to carry home your treasures.

Buttons and Beads—available from garage sales, estate sales, thrift shops, and friends. Many of these sources will give them to you for free when they know they will be used for young children.

Collage Items—those sundry materials that run from bottle caps to nuts, from sequins to broken jewelry. This will be your most valuable collection and one of the most fun to search out. Ask friends and family to save collage items for you!

Note: Always observe safety and caution with young children when using small objects, sharp objects, heat, and anything else that may be dangerous without proper supervision

General Art Materials

Stock up on the basics. Usually the more you buy, the better price you receive. The following list of general art materials will give you an idea of what to purchase and plan for. Supplies are listed alphabetically with the most basic "can't live without it" supplies starred with an *. All of these wonderful supplies are indispensable, but if you must budget and choose carefully, buy the starred items first.

A

aluminum foil
*art tissue paper

B

beeswax
bells
bowls

C

camera and film
carpentry table
clay tools
clear craft coat paint
clear plastic wrap
clothes hangers
*coffee filter
*colored chalk
*colored markers
colored sand
*construction paper
containers for paint and water
*cornstarch
corrugated cardboard
*cotton swabs
cotton balls
craft paper

craft tape
crayon sticks
*crayons
*crepe paper
cutting board

D

darning needles, plastic
doilies
dot art markers
double-sided tape
*drinking straws

E

*easel
egg dye
elastic string
*embroidery floss
enamel paint, washable
eyedroppers

F

face makeup
facial tissues
feathers
felt squares
*flour

fluorescent paper, pens, paint
foil papers
*food coloring

G

garden tools
*glitter
glitter-glue
*good, sharp scissors

H

hammer and nails (with help)
hand saw (with help)
highlight pens
hot glue gun (adults only)

I

ink, soluble, nontoxic

L

large paper
*library tape
*liquid starch

M

magazines
magnetic strips

magnifying glass
*masking tape
*measuring cups and spoons
*modeling clay
*moist clay

N

nail polish, red and clear

O

*oven
overhead projector

P

packing materials
*paintbrushes
paintbrushes, easel
paintbrushes, fine point
paintbrushes, wide
paintbrushes, watercolor
paintbrushes, house
paintbrushes, soft
paper chains, precut in strips
*paper clips
paper cups
paper hole punches
paper plates
*paper punch
*paper towels
papier-mâché paste
paraffin
*paste
*pencils and pens
permanent markers

petroleum jelly
pinking shears
*pipe cleaners
plastic tubs
plasticine
*play clay
polymer clay, such as Fimo
pompoms

R

record player
ribbon
rolling pins
rubber stamps
rubber bands

S

*salt
self-adhesive paper
sequins
*sewing trims
shells
shipping tape
spoons
*stickers
stirring sticks
string, twine, rope
sugar

T

*tape
*tempera paint, liquid
*tempera paint, powdered
thread

tiles
tools, such as screwdriver

V

varnish
vegetable dye

W

wallpaper
watercolor paint
water table, sand table
*white glue
wicky-tape (surveyor's tape)
*wire, telephone
wood shapes, blocks
wooden dowels
wooden sticks
wrapping paper

X

X-acto knife (adult only)

Y

yarn

PART 1

I've Just Begun...
Exploring Counting

CHAPTER 1

Almost Counting, One Is One

Math concepts explored in this chapter

One-to-one correspondence
Measuring materials
Counting
Shape recognition
Matching

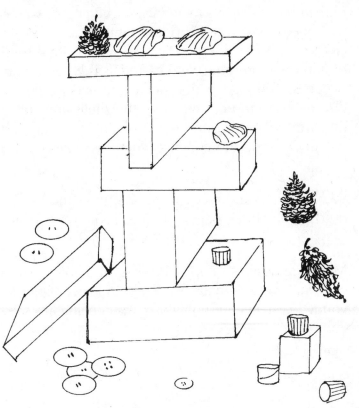

One of the first concepts a child will encounter before progressing to higher levels of mathematical thinking is one-to-one correspondence, or "1-to-1." One-to-one correspondence can easily be explored through art experiences. For example, gluing one cotton ball on one red circle (and not a handful of cotton balls all over a paper with a red circle) shows the child has a concept of the correspondence between one cotton ball and one red circle. Understanding and using the idea that one object goes with another one object is understanding one-to-one correspondence, a predecessor to counting and knowing number value.

Discrete materials are countable objects such as shells, bottle caps, pinecones, blocks, or buttons. Exploration with discrete materials gives the young learner experience handling and manipulating "pieces" and "items" that could be counted or are countable. Before a child can count, experience with countable materials prepares the child's mind for the concept of counting.

Continuous materials are measurable and have mathematical attributes, such as, they can be poured, weighed, or measured. Examples of continuous materials include water, sand, or flour. Exploration with continuous materials gives the young learner experience handling and manipulating items that prepare the child's mind to accept and understand the mathematical concepts of weighing and measuring.

The concept of conservation means that an item remains the same regardless of the shape or the arrangement of that item. For example, with continuous materials, if one cup of water is poured into a large jar, the water may look like less, but it is still one cup. When that one cup of water is poured into a small jar, the water may fill the jar and look like a lot of water, but it is still one cup. Very young children who have not mastered conservation think the little jar overflowing with water has more water than the big jar. An example of conservation of discrete materials is when a handful of shells is grouped close together or far apart. There are still the same number of shells; nothing has really changed except the arrangement of the shells. Young children may think that when the shells are spread out there are more, and when the shells are close together, there are less. Understanding the concept of conservation will occur naturally from exploring and manipulating math and art materials. If children have mathart experiences like the ones in this chapter, they will understand the concept when they are developmentally ready.

Working with and recognizing shapes is another basic math area that lends itself beautifully to creative art experiences. Shapes can be used in matching, pairs, patterns, sequences, order, and nearly all areas of math for young children.

Matching designs, shapes, objects, and colors is a beginning skill that precedes sorting and classifying. Hands-on math experiences with matching prepares the child to learn higher level math skills. Part of the matching experience is finding pairs. Some of the words young learners commonly use in matching are same, match, alike, look the same, matches, matching.

Bottle Cap Treasures

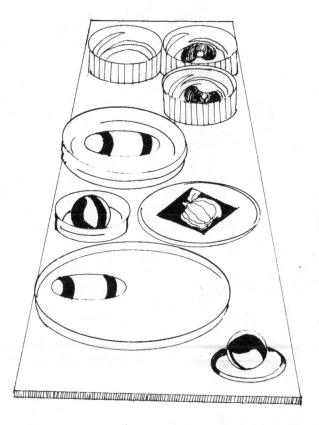

caution ◔ **3+**

one-to-one correspondence
collage

As the child explores placing one item in one container, he is learning the skill of one-to-one correspondence, which means that the child will understand the concept of one.

Materials
✓ save caps and lids from any of the following containers
      plastic milk jugs, mayonnaise jars, juice bottles, pill bottles,
      peanut butter jars, soda bottles, spice jars
✓ white glue
✓ cardboard, any size, for base of collage (big cardboard for a really big collage, small piece for small collage)
✓ a special treasure to place inside each lid or cap, such as
      stickers, small drawings, small magazine pictures, marbles, paint chips,
      flowers (pressed in wax paper), beads, photos, collections of things
Note: Use caution with young children who still put small objects in their mouths.

Process
1. Glue the caps or lids to the cardboard with the inside of the cap or lid facing up like a small cup or bowl. Completely cover the cardboard with bottle caps or jar lids touching.
2. Choose treasures to glue inside the caps or lids. Glue one treasure inside each one.
3. Dry the Bottle Cap Treasure collage overnight.

Variations
■ Cover the cardboard with wrapping paper before adding the lids and treasures.
■ Paint the cardboard, dry completely, and then glue lids and treasures to the dry, painted cardboard.

5

one-to-one correspondence collage

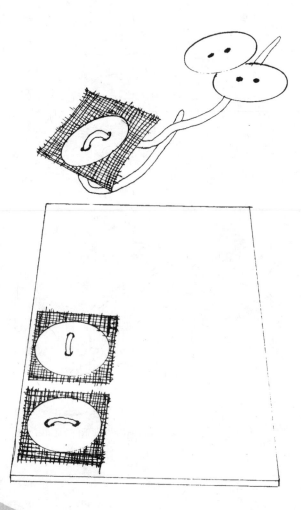

Button Sew Collage

One button on one square is a creative exploration for learning one-to-one correspondence, a prerequisite to counting.

Materials

✓ burlap cut in 20 squares, one for each button
✓ buttons with large holes, one for each square (If large-holed buttons are not available, make colorful, heavy paper circles or shapes that resemble two-holed buttons.)
✓ yarn cut in 1 foot lengths, one for each button
✓ plastic darning needle
✓ matte board or cardboard
✓ white glue or masking tape
✓ framing matte (optional)

Process

1. Thread the plastic darning needle with a piece of yarn. (For very young artists, double the yarn and knot both loose ends together.)
2. Push the needle and yarn up through a square of burlap.
3. Then push the needle through one hole in the button. Pull through.
4. Now take the needle and yarn back through the second button hole and back through the burlap. Tie or sew the yarn to the back of the burlap.
5. Continue making as many burlap squares with one button each as desired.
6. After sewing buttons on squares, glue a button square in the corner of the matte board. Masking tape works too.
7. Next glue another button square right next to the first button square, another next to that one, and so on. Fill the matte board with squares and buttons.
8. Dry completely.
9. Frame with a framing matte, if desired, using glue or tape.

Variations

■ Sew other items with holes to the burlap squares, such as pipe cleaner loops, washers and nuts, beads, small cardboard squares, telephone wire loops, homemade clay buttons.
■ Find a fabric with definite squares or circles. Sew buttons, one each to the fabric pattern square or circle.

One-to-One Nail Board

   3+

N ails are hammered into a board in any design. Then, one decorative material or item is placed on each nail. The Nail Board can be used over and
over again if decorations are removed.

**one-to-one correspondence
construction**

Materials
✓ plywood scrap or square
✓ nails
✓ hammer
✓ decorative materials or objects, such as
     nuts, washers or items with holes, ribbons, yarn, colored rubber bands,
     styrofoam packing pieces, corks, playdough balls, Plasticine modeling clay,
     plastic or silk flowers, leaves, sewing trims
✓ work surface suitable for carpentry such as a work bench

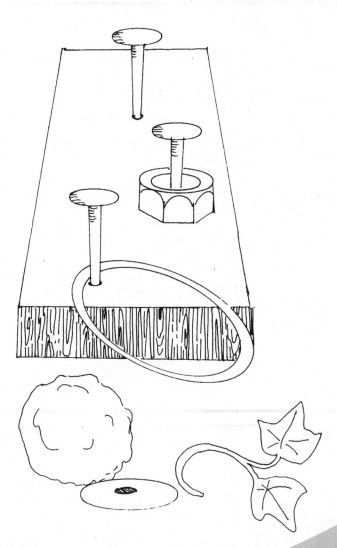

Process
1. With help from an adult, hammer nails into a scrap of wood in any fashion. Be careful that
   nails do not go through the wood into a table top or floor.
2. When nails are securely in place, begin to decorate each nail with one object or material.
   These items may be glued, tied, pressed on, or attached in any way.
3. Save the decorated sculpture, or when the artist is ready, remove the decorations and use the
   board again for a new sculpture.

Variations
■ Glue beads or sequins on each nail or to the wooden base for a sparkly sculpture.
■ Stick toothpicks or bamboo skewers into a styrofoam block and add decorative materials, one
  to each stick.
■ Place one bite of food on one toothpick and make a food sculpture. Yummy examples are
  cube of cheese, strawberry, pineapple chunk, grape, cube of turkey, banana slice.

3+ ◑ ✋

**measuring materials
drawing**

Colored Sand Drawings

Children learn how to pour the sand and about measuring and estimating with sand.

Materials
- ✓ clean, white sand
- ✓ measuring containers and cups in many sizes
- ✓ large tub or sand table
- ✓ newspaper
- ✓ powdered tempera paints in several colors or crushed chalk
- ✓ plastic spoons, stirring sticks
- ✓ plastic picnic condiment squeeze containers
- ✓ base for sand drawing, such as
      smooth playground or dirt area out of doors,
      white sheet, double or queen size
- ✓ big piece of butcher paper

Process
1. Fill a tub or sand table with clean, white sand. With a variety of measuring cups and other containers, explore pouring and measuring the sand.
2. After exploring for some time, fill several containers half full with white sand. Leave some room to mix in powdered tempera paint.
3. Scoop about one teaspoon of powdered tempera paint or crushed colored chalk per cup of sand. Use a different color of paint for each cup of sand.
4. Stir the sand and powdered paint together until the sand is thoroughly colored. Fill plastic picnic condiment squeeze containers with the colored sand, one color in each container.
5. Choose a base for the sand drawing depending on the weather, the number of children involved, and the amount of sand that is colored.
6. Squeeze colored sand in designs on the white paper. Feel free to mix sand colors into each other and cross over colors in designs on the paper.
7. When the design is complete, leave it on the paper for a time. Then, with a person holding each corner of the paper, fold the paper in half and pour all the sand into one bucket or container to use for a colored sand project.

8

Salty Painting

**measuring materials
painting**

Salt is sifted through fingers and poured by fistfuls over a glue design or draw-ing. This math activity enables children to explore quantity and measuring.

Materials

✓ 5 pounds of table salt emptied in a plastic tub
✓ white glue
✓ strong, bright food coloring mixed with water in cups or liquid watercolor paints
✓ paintbrushes for each cup
✓ eyedroppers for each cup (optional)
✓ matte board
✓ newspaper to cover work space

Process

1. Pour the bag of table salt into the plastic tub. (Rock salt can also be used. Sugar works too, but might be a little too sweet and tempting for young children.)
2. Put both hands into the tub, pouring and feeling the salt. After exploring the salt, brush hands off and begin the Salty Painting.
3. First, draw a glue design with a squeeze bottle of white glue on a hard painting surface, such as reused matte board from a framing shop. Create swirls, lines, shapes, or other designs.
4. Before the glue dries, place the entire design in the tub of salt, design side up. Try not to tip it too much or the glue will run off.
5. With hands, pour handfuls of salt over the glue design until covered. Then lift the design from the tub and let the salt that did not stick fall back into the tub.
6. With a paintbrush filled with lots of water and food coloring or paint, gently touch the tip of the brush to the salt-and-glue design. Observe how the color absorbs and travels through the salt. (An eyedropper filled with color may also be used. Drop little drops on the salt-and-glue design and observe.)
7. When the design is complete, dry for several hours. When dry, the salty design may crack and fall off the matte board, but should hold well if the board stays flat and is handled gently.

Variation

■ After coloring the salt and glue design, add more glue and more salt to the design for a very thick and puffy design.

9

3+

**measuring materials
construction**

Fancy Water Jars

Children love to pour water and explore the qualities of water. After they have explored on their own, add measuring containers, small jars, and eventually food coloring to color the jars of water.

Materials
✓ pouring area, such as a sink, water table, or plastic tub on a covered table or floor
✓ large transparent containers, such as liter bottles or gallon jugs
✓ water
✓ food coloring
✓ measuring cups
✓ small jars of various sizes with lids
✓ glitter, metallic confetti, or similar items, such as sequins
✓ duct tape

Process
1. Fill large containers with water.
2. Add food coloring to change the water in each container to a different color.
3. Explore pouring colored water into measuring cups and into small jars of various sizes.
4. When satisfied with exploring the pouring process, fill several small jars with a desired color of water.
5. Add bits of glitter, metallic confetti, or similar items, such as sequins, to the colored water.
6. Replace lid and tighten. Seal the edge of the lid to the jar with duct tape as an extra precaution.

Variations
■ Shake the jar, roll it, or turn it upside down to increase the movement of the jar's contents.
■ Fill jars with other measurable materials such as goldfish bowl gravel, coins, or paper clips.

Button Box

The children decorate and design boxes for storage of buttons, which are countable and pourable, creating permanent storage containers for sorting, grouping, and counting materials.

Materials
✓ colored paper
✓ tape or white glue
✓ empty cardboard boxes, such as
      shoe box
      cereal box
      cornmeal container
      oatmeal container
✓ crayons, markers, paints, pencils, and other drawing tools
✓ buttons
Note: Use caution with young children who still put small object in their mouths.

Process
1. Draw on colored paper with the drawing tools.
2. Cover the cardboard container with decorated colored paper, and tape or glue the seam to hold.
3. Fill the boxes with buttons of all kinds.
4. Explore counting, sorting, and grouping buttons.
5. Choose a selection of buttons to glue on the outside of the container in any design.

Variations
■ String buttons on yarn for a necklace or garland.
■ Decorate boxes with scraps of fabric or paper.

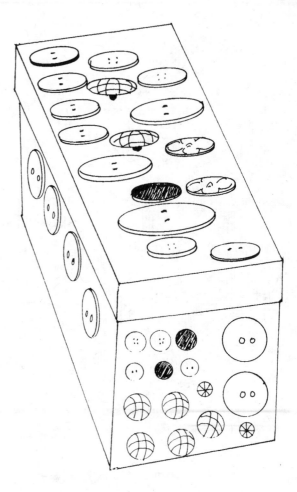

**counting
craft**

Treasure Box

Part of learning to count is exploring the process of sorting and manipulating little items into different containers.

Materials

✓ assorted boxes with lids, such as lightweight gift boxes and jewelry boxes
✓ drawing and painting materials to decorate boxes
✓ countable treasures to place in boxes, such as
       small cars, acorns,
       pinecones, washers,
       bolts and nuts,
       spools, beads, shells,
       toy parts, pebbles, seed pods
✓ white glue
✓ colored markers
Note: Use caution with young children who still put small objects in their mouths.

Process

1. Decorate assorted boxes with drawing and painting materials.
2. Fill the boxes with countable items such as pinecones, beads, or toy cars.
3. Explore the items through counting and grouping.
4. When satisfied with the counting and grouping experience, further decorate the boxes by gluing some of the smaller, flatter countable items to the box. Or, draw on the box with markers.
5. Keep special counting treasures in the Treasure Boxes.

Variations

■ Use glitter and fabric to cover and decorate Treasure Boxes.
■ Decorate boxes according to what is inside them, for example, by drawing pictures of bolts and nuts on the Treasure Box filled with bolts and nuts, or glue bolts and nuts on the treasure box filled with bolts and nuts.
■ Hide Treasure Boxes for a Treasure Box Hunt.

Little Twig Bundles

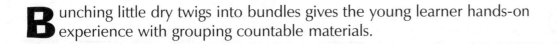

Bunching little dry twigs into bundles gives the young learner hands-on experience with grouping countable materials.

Materials
✓ string, twine, ribbon, strips of fabric, twist ties, rubber bands, pipe cleaners
✓ little twigs gathered from outdoors
✓ sticks
✓ fabric square, about 12" x 12", or a cotton bandanna
✓ paints and brushes (optional)

Process
1. First be sure twigs are clean and dry.
2. Group the twigs into little bundles and secure with ribbon, string, twine, or rubber bands. (Young children may need help with the tying.)
3. Explore twig bundles by untying and counting, arranging, grouping, and stacking.
4. Open the fabric square and spread it out on the table.
5. Place bundles of little twigs inside the fabric square.
6. Fold the fabric around the bundles in any fashion, and tie with another ribbon or strip of fabric to form a decorative bundle.
7. Use this larger bundle of twigs as a decoration, a gift, or to save and explore later for other counting activities.

Variations
■ Make popsicle stick bundles or pipe cleaner bundles.
■ Dip the end of a twig in paint. Draw with the paint dipped twig, or let the paint dry and then draw on wet paper.
■ Little Twig Bundles make a nice gift to use as a "fire-starter" for people who love camping or for the household fireplace (with supervision of course).

13

**counting
costruction**

Bright Wooden Sticks

By first grouping the sticks and then building a sculpture with them, the young artist experiences counting as well as noticing differences in color.

Materials

✓ wooden coffee stir sticks or craft sticks
✓ other wooden sticks, such as tongue depressors or medical spatulas (optional)
✓ liquid watercolor paints or food coloring (concentrated forms from hobby, craft, or grocery stores)
✓ warm water in a 9" x 13" baking pan
✓ paper towels, newspaper
✓ tongs or spatula
✓ materials to hold sticks together, such as
　　　white glue
　　　rubber bands
　　　tape

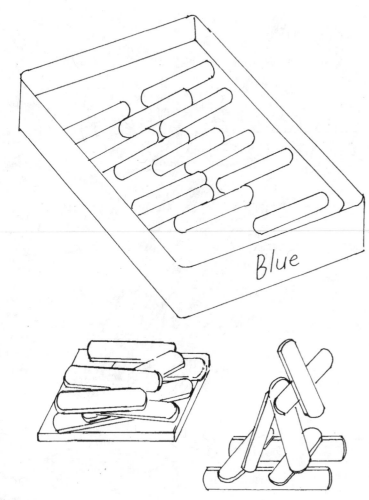

Blue

Process

1. Mix the watercolor paints or concentrated food coloring in warm water in a baking pan. Make a separate pan for each color.
2. Place wooden sticks in the warm dye. Cover the sticks completely with dye.
3. Remove the sticks with the tongs or spatula and place them on the newspaper to dry overnight.
4. When dry, explore the colored sticks by bundling, grouping, sorting, stacking, and arranging them in a variety of ways.
5. When satisfied with the exploration, sticks may be glued or joined together in designs or as a sculpture. A design may be glued flat to cardboard or paper or may be three-dimensional as shown in the illustration.

Variations

■ Holiday Wooden Stick Sculptures may be decorated with stickers, bits of colored paper, sewing trims, lace, glitter, or other collage items.
■ Build a colorful house sculpture or object with Bright Wooden Sticks.
■ Sort Bright Wooden Sticks by color, size, shape, or other attributes. Then glue them to a piece of wood or cardboard showing the sorting in the glued down design.

Shape Rub Resist

  3+

Making a crayon rubbing of paper shapes is a tactile experience that reinforces and strengthens the children's learning so they can remember shapes through the sense of touch.

Materials

✓ paper shapes, precut from heavy paper, by an adult
✓ masking tape
✓ peeled crayons
✓ flat cookie sheet or tray with no sides
✓ wide soft brush
✓ paint wash in a jar
   Note: A paint wash is tempera paint thinned with water. Watercolor paint, vegetable dye, or food coloring can also be used.
✓ drawing paper
✓ newspaper for drying area

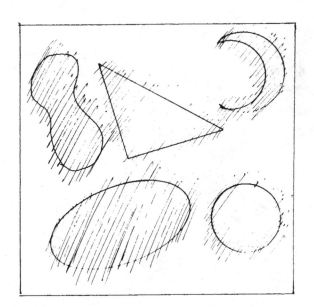

Process

1. Place a paper shape on the tray or cookie sheet.
2. Place a piece of paper over the shape. Tape the corners to the tray to prevent the paper from wiggling, if needed.
3. With a peeled crayon, rub over the shape until the design appears. Coloring hard and bright is encouraged.
4. Lift one corner of the paper and move the shape slightly.
5. With a different color of crayon (or same color) rub over the shape again.
6. Lift the corner of the paper and move the shape again. Make another rubbing.
7. Continue making rubbings of the moved shape until satisfied with the design.
8. Brush a paint wash over the crayon rubbing for added artistic effect.
9. Remove from the tray and dry on newspaper.

Variations

■ Trace a shape with crayon. Brush over the tracings with a paint wash.
■ Combine tracings and rubbings in one design.
■ Paste shapes on the completed Shape Rub Resist.
■ Create a shape rub with more than one shape, grouping and overlapping matching shapes.

15

shape recognition
printing

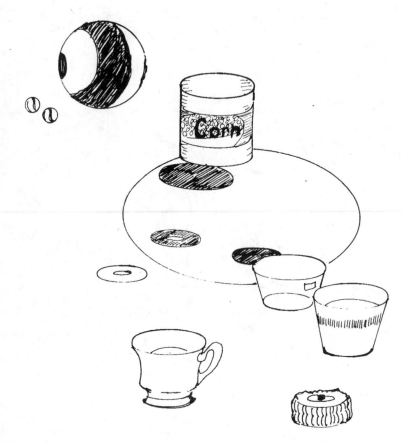

Shape on Shape Print

Printing an ink shape on a matching paper shape requires the math skill of matching and the artistic skill of creating a design.

Materials
✓ 9" x 12" paper, cut in shapes
✓ objects to make shape prints, on a tray, such as
      parts of toys, blocks, kitchen utensils, tools, hardware items,
          odds and ends, homemade stamps, shapes cut from cardboard
✓ ink pads in a variety of colors
✓ table covered with butcher paper for practice printing

Process
1. Precut the paper into a shape, such as a circle, square, or triangle.(Use adult help, if necessary.) With young children, start with one shape.
2. Assemble objects that make shape prints, such as a cylinder block that makes a circle print or the base of a small box that makes a square. Find about four items in each shape, if possible.
3. Press an object on the ink pad. Then practice pressing it on the butcher paper covering the table to see if it is a shape that will match the shape paper.
4. If the shape print is the same shape as the paper shape, press the object on the ink pad again, then press on the paper. For example, make a circle print with the cylinder block on the circle paper (but set aside a square block that does not match the circle paper).
5. Explore the printing objects, finding those that make prints to match the shape paper and make as many prints and designs as desired.
6. If desired, have other cut-out shapes of paper ready at the same time, such as squares and triangles to accept the prints of those objects that make matching prints. Then the artist can make prints with all the objects.

Variations
■ Make a blank book in the shape of a circle, square, or triangle. Place shapes that match in the book, such as prints, cutouts, and drawings. Each page can have a different kind of art showing the matching shape of the book.
■ Cut newsprint in a shape and place it at the easel. Artists paint shapes or any painting on the shaped paper.

Living Shape Sculpture

A group of at least four children is needed to create a group shape using their own bodies as the art medium of the sculpture.

Materials
✓ at least 3 children
✓ other children to watch and take turns
✓ open area such as a grassy yard or carpeted floor
✓ shapes cut from heavy paper or cardboard

Process
1. First, look at, examine, and feel a cardboard shape such as a square or triangle.
2. Next, with the children working together, get down on the floor and form that shape using the four bodies to create the shape (like drawing lines on paper).
3. The observers can see if the "human shape" matches the cardboard shape.
4. Repeat this experience with a different shape. (Shapes may also be created with children standing, although this is more difficult.)

Variations
■ Take a photograph of the human shapes so the artists can view their creations.
■ Make a masking tape shape or form a rope shape on the carpet. Ask children to lie down on the carpet following the shape with their bodies.
■ Draw shapes on a chalk board with fingers dipped in water.
■ Paint shapes on a chalk board with a paintbrush dipped in water.

17

3+

matching
drawing

Rub and Trace Shape Match

Two crayon techniques combine to make a visually interesting matching design from one stencil.

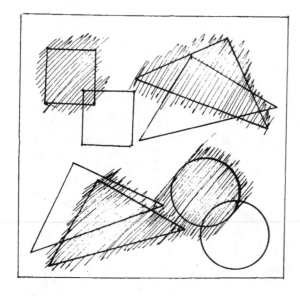

Materials
✓ stencils of shapes (circle, square, triangle) precut by an adult from heavy paper, matte or tag board
✓ drawing paper or butcher paper
✓ peeled crayons
✓ markers or other drawing tools
✓ tape

Process
1. Select a stencil shape that has been cut from heavy paper or matte board. Place it on the table.
2. Place the drawing paper over the shape. (Tape the corners of the paper to the table to stop the paper from wiggling.) Rub over the shape with a peeled crayon held on its side. Rub hard and bright. Watch for a complete shape to emerge. Use more than one color, if desired, or a multicolored "scribble cookie."
3. Next, bring the shape out from under the paper and place on top of the paper.
4. Using any drawing tool (marker, crayon, pencil, pen), trace around the shape.
5. Remove the stencil and two shapes will be visible: one from the rubbing and one from the tracing.
6. Repeat the rubbing and tracing with the same shape, a different shape, or leave the artwork as in its present form.

Variations
■ Paint over the crayon rubbing and tracing with a thin wash of tempera paint.
■ Trace shapes and paint or color them to match.

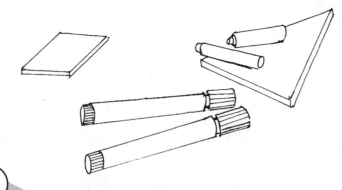

18

Matching Block Sculpture

Tracing blocks on the inside lid of a box is the beginning of matching objects to their own shapes in this wood sculpture activity.

Materials
✓ wooden blocks and wood scraps with shapes such as squares, circles, triangles
✓ lid of shirt or coat box
✓ markers
✓ paints and brushes
✓ white glue
✓ glitter, confetti (optional)

Process
1. Place the box lid on the table with the inside as the work surface.
2. Choose a block or scrap and place it in the lid. Trace the block with a marker.
3. Choose another block and trace it, keeping the shapes separate.
4. Trace shapes until satisfied or until the lid is filled. Shapes should not overlap.
5. With paint or markers, further draw on the tracing lines to make them bright and visible.
6. Make the lines wider and bolder than before so the colors will show. Dry, if paint was used.
7. Find the block or scrap that matches one of the traced shapes and glue it on the tracing. The color will surround the base of the shape if wide, bold lines were made.
8. Glue all the matching wood scraps on their matching traced shapes. Dry.
9. Paint the wooden blocks in the sculpture or leave them as they are.
10. Decorate the wooden blocks with glitter or confetti, for extra decoration.

Variation
■ Make ink prints of sponges, corks, and other odds and ends. Then glue the objects to their actual matching print.

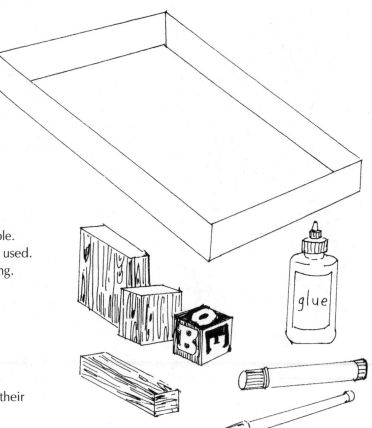

3+ ◗ ⊛

**matching
sculpture**

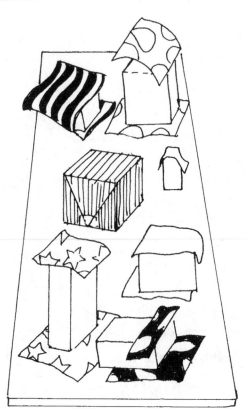

Wrap Scrap Match

Add scraps of wrapping paper and gift wrap to a wood scrap collage to give young learners a creative experience finding matching patterns.

Materials
✓ gift wrap scraps in a shallow box
✓ small wood scraps
✓ scissors
✓ white glue
✓ cardboard for base of sculpture
✓ newspaper-covered work area

Process
1. Spread the wood scraps out on the table with the box of gift wrap scraps. Place the cardboard base nearby.
2. With adult help, trim gift wrap to a manageable size and glue it to the face of a wood scrap. Extra paper can be glued down around the edges of the scrap or trimmed away.
3. Glue a piece of the same gift wrap to the piece of cardboard base.
4. Continue gluing scraps of wrapping paper on the wood pieces and then a matching piece of wrap on the cardboard.
5. When satisfied with the wood scraps and cardboard, join the two together.
6. Glue the wood scrap on or near the matching paper on the cardboard.
7. Continue until all the wood scraps have found a matching paper scrap. Dry completely.

Variation
■ Glue squares of gift wrap to a piece of cardboard. Then glue small matching scraps of the same patterns on the large squares.

Copycat Partner Patterns

Each artist takes turns gluing a colorful shape on one side of the paper. Then the partner copies the placement of an identical shape on the other side of the paper.

Materials
✓ heavy paper folded in half the long way, then unfolded
✓ sticky-dots
✓ precut paper shapes
✓ white glue or tape
✓ small table and two chairs

Process
1. Fold and unfold a heavy sheet of paper the long way.
2. Place it on the small table for two, stretching from left to right.
3. Place a chair on either side of the table so the friends are facing each other.
4. One artist attaches a sticky-dot or shape to her side of the paper.
5. The other artist copies the placement and the choice of shape on his side of the paper. (Artists can take turns deciding who places the next shape, or they can work together as they go.)
6. The two artists continue to add shapes and sticky-dots until they have a copycat pattern with a matching design that they like.

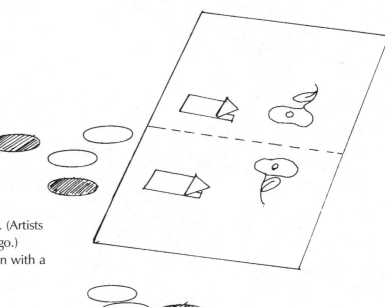

Variations
- One artist creates a completed pattern on one side of the folded paper. The challenge comes for the second artist who copies the first pattern after the fact.
- Stick tissue paper shapes and colors on clear self-adhesive paper.
- Stick tissue paper shapes and colors on paper with liquid starch.
- Use collage materials instead of shapes or sticky-dots.

3+ ◐

**matching
collage**

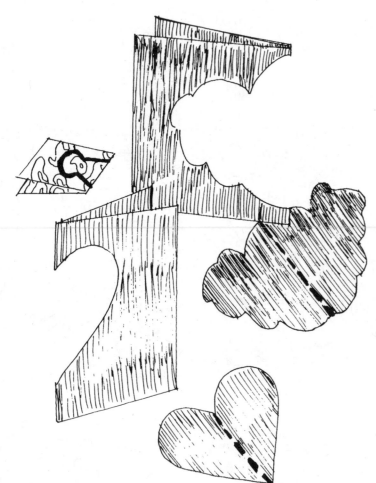

Missing Matching Paste-Up

Matching missing paper cutouts reinforces the skill of noticing similarities and differences of shapes.

Materials
✓ any of the following papers, such as
      scraps of construction paper
      wallpaper
      wrapping paper
      scrap paper
✓ scissors
✓ box for storage of shapes and scraps
✓ white glue
✓ piece of butcher paper (poster size)

Process
1. Choose a paper scrap and fold it in half.
2. Cut out any shape on the fold line. Most young artists create unusual shapes rather than circles, squares, and triangles.
3. Open the folded scrap and place in a box. Place the cut-out shape in the box too.
4. Cut as many shapes from folded scraps as desired.
5. When sufficient shapes and scraps have been placed in the box, the collage is ready to create and assemble.
6. Spread out all the cut-out shapes and their unfolded matching scraps. Find two that match.
7. Glue them on the poster-sized butcher paper. They can be glued like a puzzle piece inside the space, or they can be glued like pairs or partners. Overlapping shapes is effective too.
8. Add more missing matching shapes to the cut-out form. It is not necessary to use all the shapes and scraps, but it is fine to do so.
9. Dry the matching shapes poster.

Variation
■ Use the matching shapes and cutouts for a design on a long, narrow piece of paper that goes around the room.

22

Exploring Counting

Many Kinds of Many Kinds

Math concepts explored in this chapter

Sorting and classifying

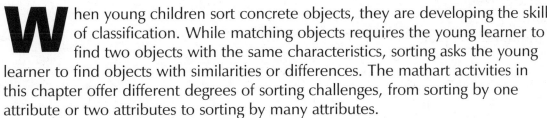

When young children sort concrete objects, they are developing the skill of classification. While matching objects requires the young learner to find two objects with the same characteristics, sorting asks the young learner to find objects with similarities or differences. The mathart activities in this chapter offer different degrees of sorting challenges, from sorting by one attribute or two attributes to sorting by many attributes.

Classifying is sorting objects into groups or categories, a step up from simple sorting. The activities in this chapter encourage children to invent their own categories for sorting and to develop an eye for detail in differences and similarities. Some of the concepts in the sorting and classifying activities are sort, group, color names, match, put together, alike, different, not the same, one, some, many, all, none, no, not. Collect a wide and interesting variety of objects for mathart activities and creative sorting will begin!

Words young learners use when sorting and classifying are based on the five senses and how they perceive things with those senses.

Feeling
scratchy — smooth
warm — cool
hard — soft
slippery —sticky
dry — wet
thick — thin
bumpy — smooth

Sight
little — big
large — small
long — short
shiny — dull
curvy — straight
round — square
bright — pastel
color names — shapes names

Smelling
bad — good
sweet — bitter
flowery — stinky

Sound
low — high
loud — soft
pretty — ugly
nice — mean

Tasting
bad — good
yukky — yummy
salty — sweet
bland — bitter
mmmmmmm—plain

Other words and observations could include: noticing art materials that are made of wood, plastic, paper, metal, cardboard, or yarn; or noticing qualities and measurements of art materials such as, lots of glue, thinner paint, more paste, thicker fabric.

Surprise Table

3+

T his type of project should be experienced several times as children catch on
to the possibilities of hiding objects and shapes and then making crayon rubbings of them.

Materials

✓ any flat items to create textured surprises, such as
    sand paper, rubber bands, paper clips, yarn,
    confetti, stencils, paper shapes, leaves
✓ a smooth table at child height
✓ large sheet of butcher paper, light color preferred
✓ peeled jumbo crayons, or any crayons
✓ masking tape

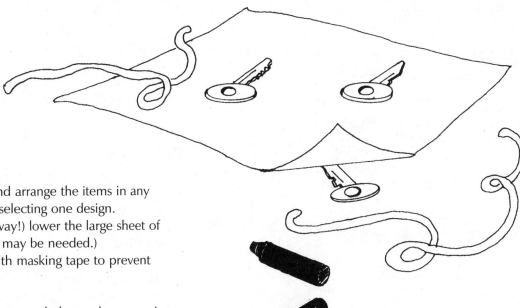

Process

1. Spread all the flat textured surprise items on the table. Sort and arrange the items in any
design. Feel free to move them around over and over before selecting one design.
2. Carefully (don't cause too much "wind" and blow them all away!) lower the large sheet of
butcher paper over the surprises and cover them. (Adult help may be needed.)
3. Tape the corners and other edges of the paper to the table with masking tape to prevent
slipping (and peeking).
4. Invite others to the Surprise Table who did not design it.
5. With peeled crayons held on their sides, begin rubbing the paper and observe how surprises
appear from the rubbing. Feel the paper with hands to be sure all the hidden surprises have
been exposed by the crayon rubbings.
6. Leave the Surprise Table just as it is to enjoy as a fancy table decoration or remove it for a wall
decoration.

Variations

- Use the large rubbing as wrapping paper, cutting it into smaller pieces, if needed.
- Use the rubbing for a crayon resist by painting over the crayon rubbing with watercolor paints
or thinned tempera paints.

25

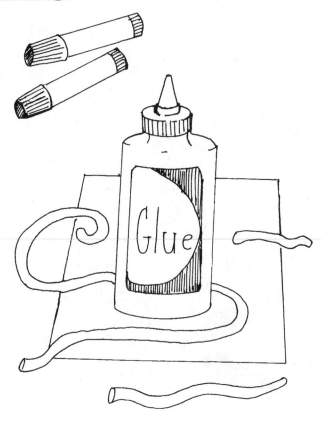

Yarn, Piece by Piece

Sorting yarn pieces by their lengths to use in a drawing collage activity is a beginning exploration of measuring.

Materials
✓ yarn in assorted colors and lengths (scraps are fine)
✓ scissors
✓ 3 paper envelopes
✓ crayons and markers, such as, Crayola Overwriter Pens and Changeable Pens that create unusual and magical designs
✓ matte board or construction paper
✓ white glue

Process
1. Snip yarn into a variety of lengths.
2. Sort yarn into long, medium, and short pieces.
3. Decorate the envelopes for yarn storage indicating which envelope holds long, medium, or short yarns. A piece of yarn may be glued to the envelope as an indication or label.
4. Fill each envelope with one category of the length of the yarns.
5. To create the yarn design on the matte board, "draw" with the white glue in the squeeze bottle on the matte board, going slowly and making thick designs and lines.
6. Then place one piece of yarn at a time into the glue. Dry completely, usually overnight.
7. When the yarn design is dry, draw and color between the yarn designs with crayons and markers. Color directly on the yarn pieces too.

Variation
■ Use yarn pieces to create a realistic picture such as a flower, animal or house. Fill in the design with shredded yarn, colored sand, collage items, or markers.

Circle Trace and Paint

Tracing circles and then painting them gives the young learner an experience with sorting that creates a bright, bold painting or poster.

Materials
✓ crayons or pencils
✓ items for tracing circles, such as
    bowls, jar lids, pots and pans, cardboard circles, plastic cups,
    soup cans, coffee cans, plastic container lids, stencils
✓ paper
✓ paints and brushes

Process
1. Trace cans or other items with pencils or crayons to make circles all over the paper. Create a random pattern or a planned design. (For this first experience, circles should not touch each other. In later experiences, circles may overlap each other.)
2. Choose a paint color and paint a group of circles.
3. Choose a second paint color and paint a different group of circles.
4. Continue choosing and painting, or stop at two colors.
5. Dry.

Variations
- Make other shapes such as triangles, octagons, or invented shapes.
- Make shapes in assorted sizes (small, medium, and large) paint the small shapes one color, the medium shapes another color, and the large shapes yet another color.

3+

Shape and Color Print

The sponge printing of shapes gives the artist an opportunity to manipulate the sorting in his own way while creating a sponge print artwork.

Materials
✓ sponge pieces cut into 3 shapes (circle, square, and triangle)
✓ tempera paints in 3 colors (such as red, blue, and yellow), each in a flat styrofoam tray
✓ paper for printing
✓ newspaper-covered table or work space

Process
1. Begin by selecting one sponge shape. Make a print with that shape with each color, spreading out the prints so there is space between them. Color will be the important factor for the rest of the printing.
2. Next, select a second shape. Make prints with that shape, trying to group the prints by color. For example, print the blue square near the blue circle. Print the red triangle near the red square and red circle.
3. There will be a group of red shapes, a group of blue shapes and a group of yellow shapes when the printing is complete.
4. The resulting print shows groups of shapes in three colors.

Variations
■ With young children use one shape and two colors, or two shapes and two colors.
■ Use shapes cut out of wallpaper patterns. Sort and glue into a collage.
■ Use shapes cut out of felt or fabric. Sort and glue into a collage.

Stamp Block Design

Printing with one shape over and over with different colors of paint allows the young learner to look at sorting one shape according to color.

Materials
✓ block of wood
✓ poster board
✓ white glue
✓ tempera paints
✓ scissors
✓ paper
✓ styrofoam tray
✓ facial tissues

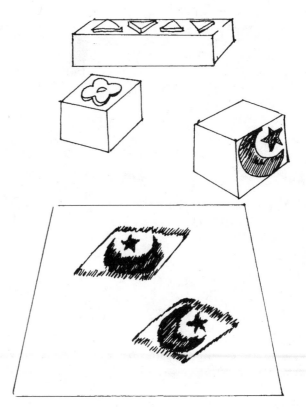

Process
Make the stamp block
1. Cut out shapes from the poster board that will be small enough to fit on the wooden block.
2. Glue small shapes onto one side of the block. Set aside to dry completely.
Use the stamp block and make the design
3. Place a puddle of one color of paint in the styrofoam tray.
4. Dip the block stamp into the paint.
5. Press the stamp onto paper to create an original design.
6. Repeat several times.
7. With paper towels or tissues, wipe paint from the block stamp before selecting a new paint color for stamping.
8. Dip the block stamp into another color and continue printing. Make prints in groups of similar colors or put into designs of similar colors.
9. Completed designs may be sorted by the same design or same color.

Variations
■ Make more than one block stamp to use with different colors of paint. Then it is not necessary to clean stamps between colors.
■ Make stamps using triangles, circles, and rectangles as a theme.

29

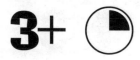
**sorting
sculpture**

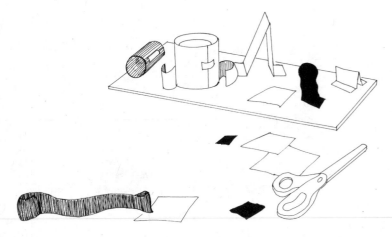

Paper Piece Sculpture

Paper Piece Sculpture challenges the young learner to manipulate and shape the pieces into a three-dimensional artwork rather than a flat collage.

Materials
✓ construction paper in assorted colors
✓ poster or tag board for a base
✓ white glue
✓ stapler
✓ tape
✓ scissors

Process
1. Cut construction paper into various shapes.
2. Sort and stack shapes by their colors.
3. Bend, curl, snip, roll, fringe, and stack paper pieces.
4. Tape and glue pieces together in three dimensional sculptures.
5. When the papers have dried some and are sticking together, staple or tape them to the poster board base.

Variations
- Paint corrugated cardboard in a bright color, let dry, cut, and create a sculpture.
- Sort handfuls of playdough by color and create a playdough sculpture.
- For a group sculpture, each child creates a Paper Piece Sculpture on an 8" x 8" piece of matte board. Join all of the sculptures into one, bringing them together on a bulletin board or table top.

Single Sort Design

Sorting out paper scraps of one color and pasting them in a collage is a hands-on way to begin sorting.

Materials

✓ box of scraps of construction paper
✓ scissors
✓ white glue or paste
✓ base for the collage, such as
>   box lid
>   piece of cardboard
>   piece of matte board
>   sheet of paper

Process

1. Look in the box of colorful paper scraps. Select a color to search for, such as blue.
2. Find all the blue scraps and pull them out.
3. From the blue scraps, choose some pieces to glue to the cardboard or paper. Scraps may be cut into shapes or glued as they come from the box. Enjoy free-form cutting and pasting.
4. Dry.

Variations

■ Divide a large sheet of paper into two or four sections. Sort scraps into two or four colors and glue them in the sections of the base paper.
■ Other things may be sorted for a collage with one attribute. Shiny beads can be sorted from mixed beads glued on a styrofoam tray. Orange autumn leaves can be sorted from mixed colors glued on a styrofoam tray. Maple leaves can be sorted from mixed types glued on a piece of paper.

31

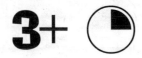

3+

sorting collage

Paper Piece Pictures

Part of the creativity of this collage is cutting the shapes; the rest is how the shapes are glued together.

Materials
✓ paper in assorted colors
✓ scissors
✓ white glue or paste
✓ plastic sandwich bags

Process
1. Cut paper of different colors into small pieces with scissors.
2. Sort pieces of paper according to likenesses in size, shape, or color.
3. Glue or paste paper pieces with similar attributes onto a paper to make a design or picture.
4. Dry.
5. Store pieces in sandwich bags for further sorting and art ideas.

Variations
- Use a hole punch to add new paper piece shapes. Many hole punch shapes are available in school supply and craft stores.
- An adult can cut paper on a paper cutter to make additional paper piece shapes.
- Using a large needle and heavy thread, string paper pieces like a garland or necklace.
- Stretch a piece of yarn across a table. Tape either end of the yarn to the table. Glue pieces of paper to the yarn. Hang from the ceiling when dry.

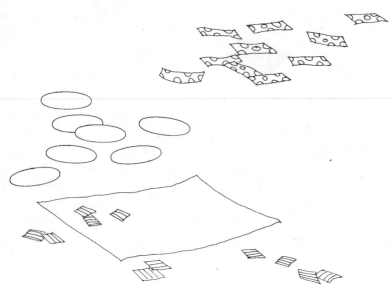

32

Paper Square Collage

Working with shapes that are all one type, such as a square, isolates the sorting challenge to color and size only.

Materials
✓ paper of any kind in assorted colors
✓ paper for base material of design, such as
      matte board
      cardboard
      construction paper
✓ scissors
✓ plastic sandwich bags or plastic snap-lid containers
✓ white glue

Process
1. Cut paper into squares of different sizes.
2. Place paper squares in a pile on the table.
3. Sort the paper squares into groups according to size or color.
4. Glue the paper squares on the matte board or cardboard in a design.

Variations
■ Cut out triangles, circles, and other shapes instead of squares.
■ Follow directions above but change what shape is used.
■ Use drawing materials to decorate paper shapes before gluing.
■ Use stickers to decorate the shapes before or after gluing.
■ Adults can use a paper cutter to create uniform sizes for the younger child.

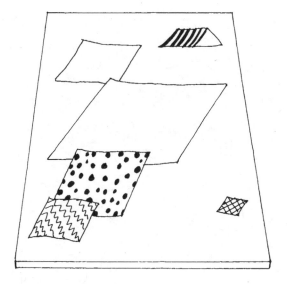

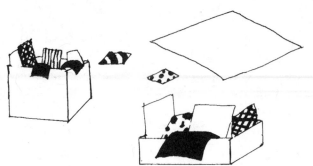

(33)

**sorting
collage**

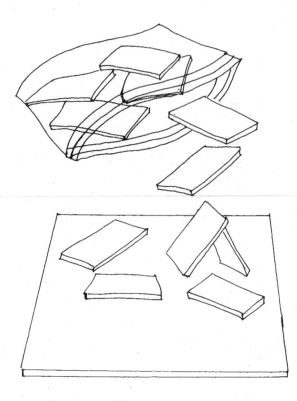

Poster Board Design

Poster board scraps can be reused by first sorting them by color and then incorporating them in a simple, bold collage. If poster board is not available, construction paper will work just fine.

Materials
✓ poster board scraps in several colors
✓ scissors
✓ lids and boxes for tracing
✓ pencil
✓ plastic sandwich bags or snap-lid containers for storage
✓ matte board or heavy paper
✓ white glue and tape

Process
1. Cut colored poster board into small shapes. Shapes may be freeform designs or more defined shapes such as circles and squares traced from lids and boxes. (Adult help may be needed.)
2. To store, place pieces of poster board in sandwich bags or plastic containers, sorted according to colors.
3. Using the poster board pieces sorted by color, create a same color design or sculpture by assembling pieces of the poster board with glue or tape on the matte board.
4. Create a permanent design or sculpture with glue, or for temporary sculptures and designs, return pieces to sandwich bags and use again.

Variations
■ Use fabric pieces instead of poster board. In addition, fabric may be glued to poster board to make it heavier and more durable for busy hands.
■ Use wallpaper scraps or construction paper instead of poster board.
■ Sort and group poster board shapes by shape, size, or thickness.

Paper Collection

Sorting paper scraps according to their likes and differences and then using those scraps in a collage is a great way to practice comparing skills.

Materials

✓ base for collection, such as
    construction paper, cardboard, matte board,
    gift boxes, smooth wood, file folder
✓ white glue or paste
✓ scissors
✓ paper, such as
    art tissue, magazine pictures, photographs, greeting cards,
    wallpaper, junk mail, wrapping paper

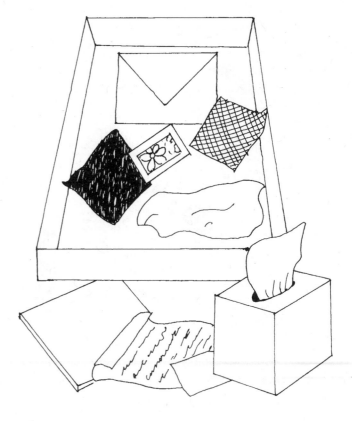

Process

1. Sort the pieces of paper until satisfied with the selection.
   Some suggestions for sorting might be
       color or texture, design on paper, type of paper,
       glossy or not, thick or thin
2. Begin gluing the selected pieces of paper according to how it was sorted, or create an entirely new design on the matte board.
3. Paint entire paper collection with a coat of white glue for a glaze.

Variations

■ Use magazine or catalog pictures to create and design a hi-tech character with a body from a computer, arms from a DVD player, feet from telephones, or any other hi-tech magazine pictures.
■ Cut greeting cards into circles only. Glue them in a pattern on a heavy base such as matte board. Fill in the spaces with other paper or leave blank.
■ Cover a sheet of cardboard with wrapping paper. Glue small squares of a different wrapping paper in a pattern or design. Use the whole sheet covered cardboard but let parts of the wrapping paper show through.

3+ ◕ ✊

**sorting
collage**

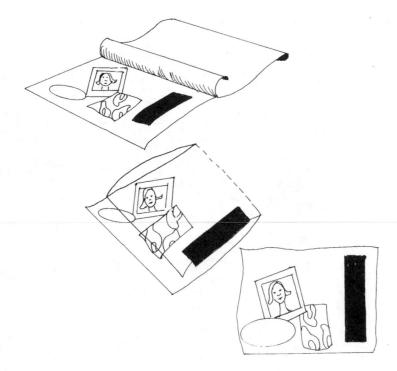

Sticky Paper Collection

Once the child understands the technique of sticking paper to the adhesive, the idea of sorting and classifying can be added to the challenge of making a collage on self-adhesive paper.

Materials
✓ any collection of paper, such as
>   art tissue in several colors, magazine pictures, photographs, wrapping paper, junk mail, greeting cards, stickers on paper, wallpaper

✓ 12" x 12" piece of clear self-adhesive paper
✓ scissors
✓ paper punch (optional)
✓ small piece of yarn or ribbon (optional)

Process
1. Collect and save paper of all sorts, textures, colors, types. Look for papers that are shiny, bumpy, patterned.
2. Cut and trim paper into shapes.
3. Explore and work with the shapes by sorting them into groups.
4. When finished exploring the paper pieces, open a piece of clear self-adhesive paper halfway. That is, pull back the protective covering halfway, exposing the sticky side to just one half. The sticky half will be the design area.
5. Begin sticking the pieces of paper directly on the sticky paper, according to the grouping or arranging, or stick the pieces of paper in any design.
6. When satisfied with the design, pull the remaining part of the sticky paper covering away. Carefully fold over the unused half over the design half. Press the sides together. Wrinkles and other sticky results are common.
7. With the scissors, trim away or shape the edges of the paper design.
8. If desired, punch a hole in the design and insert a yarn loop or tie for hanging the design in a window or near a light source.

Gatherings Collage

Young children enjoy the bigness of this outdoor collage, while exploring the math concept of sorting and the art technique of creating a collage in a large space.

Materials

✓ basket, box, or bag for gathering
✓ natural materials gathered outside, such as
    rocks, pebbles, sticks, twigs, gravel, dried weeds,
    pinecones, pine needles, dried flowers, pods,
    leaves, seeds, downed tree branches, shells,
    driftwood, grasses
✓ open area, such as yard, playground, or field

Process

1. Go for a walk outside and collect materials from nature that have fallen to the ground or are dried.
2. Bring gathered materials back to a sorting and creating area such as an open space on a playground, field, or yard.
3. Begin sorting and arranging materials on the ground.
4. Create a collage or design with the materials directly on the ground.
5. Leave the collage on the ground for awhile to enjoy, but pick up materials and tidy up the yard when finished. Clean up the outdoor collage when ready but before the wind starts to blow.

Variation

■ Collect one theme item from outdoors or one type of outdoor item to glue into a collage on cardboard or wood. Suggestions include dried flowers, weeds and seeds, autumn leaves, evergreen needles, pretty rocks.

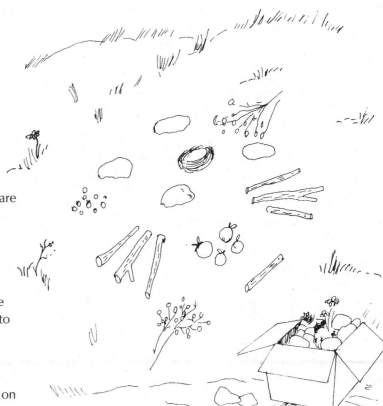

**sorting
collage**

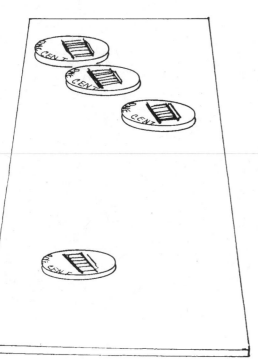

Shiny Pennies Design

By sorting coins according to their differences, the young learner compares the fronts and backs of the pennies. Provide a magnifying glass to encourage detailed discoveries.

Materials
✓ pennies
✓ masking tape
✓ poster board
✓ magnifying glass
    Note: Use caution with young children who still put small objects in their mouths.

Process
1. Place pennies in a pile on the table.
2. Explore the differences between the fronts and backs of the coins. Use a magnifying glass to see details more clearly.
3. Put little rolls or loops of masking tape on one side of each penny.
4. Press and stick the pennies on the poster board, aligning the pennies according to their differences (heads up, then tails up), or arrange pennies in a creative design.
5. After enjoying the Shiny Pennies Design for some time, remember to remove them from the poster board and save the pennies for spending, or use them for other counting, sorting, or patterning projects.

Variations
■ Before using the pennies, polish them with copper polish for an extra bright and shiny creation.
■ Use both dull and shiny pennies and sort by that characteristic.
■ Use other types of coins including foreign or game token coins.
■ With markers or paint, draw and design around the pennies with colors and markings. Fill in the poster board partially or completely.

Same and Different Collage

Creating a collage of "same and different" is a way to record the sorting as well as to create an interesting work of art.

Materials

✓ any collage items, such as
   stickers
   beads
   cotton balls
   toy parts
   scraps of paper
✓ white glue
✓ paper plate folded in half

Process

1. For the base of the collage, fold a paper plate in half then unfold. Set aside.
2. Sort collage items into two piles: things that are the same and things that are different. Some of the possibilities might be:
   Sort all buttons in one pile, everything else in the other pile.
   Sort soft materials in one pile, hard materials in the other pile.
   Sort red things in one pile, other colors in the other pile.
3. Glue all or some of the items that are the same on one side of the plate.
4. Glue all or some of the items that are different on the other side.

Variations

- By varying the collage items or varying the base, the collage can change dramatically. For instance, use a piece of plywood for the base and use a hammer and nails to attach different types of things.
- Suspend sorted items on a string or yarn from a hoop or clothes hanger to create a same and different mobile.

39

3+ ◑ ✋ (caution)

sorting collage

Button Sorting Squares

The artist sorts the buttons into two piles, sorting by one attribute such as size.

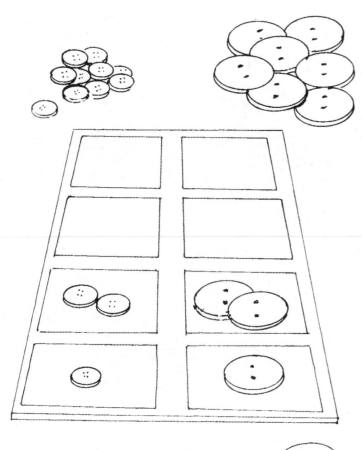

Materials

✓ 2 types of buttons, 10 identical buttons of each type (20 total)
✓ white glue
✓ squares of colored paper, about 8 squares (approximately 5" x 5")
✓ larger piece of paper (approximately 20" x 20")
✓ glitter and paint, brushes (optional)
   Note: Use caution with young children who still put small objects in their mouths.

Process

1. First place eight colorful squares of paper on the larger sheet of paper in two rows of four, or some similar pattern.
2. Sort buttons that are identical into two piles. There will be ten buttons in each pile (two piles or two kinds of buttons).
3. To make the button collage, glue one button from one pile in the first square. Glue one button from the other pile in another square.
4. Next, glue two buttons from one pile in another square, and two buttons from the other pile in another square. Then three. Then four. All the squares will be filled. Dry.
5. Paint around the designs and decorate with glitter.

Variation

■ Sort and glue other collage items or objects, such as
      used holiday decorations
      beads
      colored cotton balls

Greeting Card Sort

Pieces of recycled greeting cards are sorted by a characteristic of the artist's choosing and then assembled in a collage.

sorting collage

Materials
✓ used greeting cards in a box
✓ scissors
✓ white glue or tape
✓ small paper plates
✓ large piece of heavy paper

Process
1. Select used greeting cards from a box for sorting and making a collage.
2. Trim parts of the cards with scissors and glue or tape each one on a small paper plate.
3. Sort the greeting card designs into any chosen groups, such as birthday, big, bright, bumpy, funny, flowers.
4. When satisfied with the sorting, glue or tape the paper plates with their card designs, keeping the sorted groups together, to a large piece of heavy paper.

Variations
- Cut any of the following papers or materials for a sorting art project:
   wallpaper scraps, paper packing, colored paper scraps,
   old playing cards, wrapping paper scraps, old game cards,
   paintings and drawings, little pictures and designs
- Use any of the following materials for background instead of paper plates:
   small cardboard jewelry boxes, box lids, jar lids, styrofoam trays,
   cottage cheese and yogurt lids, pieces of cardboard, matte board

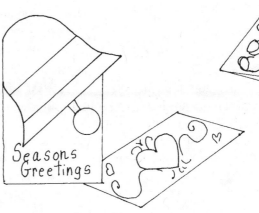

41

3+ ◐ ✋

All Sorts of Beads

The difficulty level of sorting the beads will depend on the variety of beads created and sorting experiences of the child.

Materials
✓ toothpicks
✓ yarn, string, or leather for necklace
✓ clear nail polish (optional)

Process
1. Make the bead dough recipe. Pinch off bits of dough and roll or shape into beads. Make all sorts of shapes such as cubes, cones, tubes, and balls.
2. Poke a hole in each bead with a toothpick. (Try forming beads around the toothpick instead of by hand.)
3. Stick the toothpick and bead into another leftover ball of dough or a piece of styrofoam to dry. Turn beads during drying process so they won't stick to the toothpick.
4. Dry for several days. Large or thick beads will take longer.
5. When beads are dry, coat with clear nail polish to protect, if desired. (Beads could be further decorated with markers before coating with nail polish.) Dry again.
6. When beads are completely dry, remove from the toothpicks and place on the work surface.
7. Sort and classify beads according to shapes, colors, or other chosen attributes.
8. String beads on yarn, leather, or string as a necklace or decoration. String according to how beads were sorted or make patterns from the sorted beads.

Variations
■ Make other things from dough to sort instead of beads, such as
   play food, holiday decorations, jewelry,
   flowers, bugs, doll needs, shells,
   play candy, pebbles
■ Make garlands of beads combined with other items such as paper circles, tissue scraps, cut drinking straws.

Bead Recipe
   3/4 cup flour
   1/2 cup cornstarch
   1/2 cup salt
   powdered paint or vegetable dye for color
   3/8 cup warm water
Mix flour, cornstarch, and salt in a cup or bowl. Add paint or dye to create a colored dough. To create more than one color, divide dough in parts before adding paint or dye colors. Slowly add warm water until the dough can be kneaded into a smooth, stiff dough. If too sticky, add flour.

42

CHAPTER 3

One, Two, Red, Blue

Math concepts explored in this chapter

Patterns
Sequence
Order

By the time young learners are three years old, they have experienced patterns in their world. They may have made patterns with paints or blocks, worn clothing with patterns or viewed patterns in nature. The mathart activities in chapter three build on sorting and classifying skills, helping the child learn about patterns and relationships, an essential concept for solving problems and learning in both math and art.

Young learners will continue to notice attributes, matching and sorting, and the ideas of same and different. They will recognize how attributes form patterns, how one pattern might relate to another, and how patterns repeat themselves in sequence. Order can mean first, second, third; or order can mean "from smallest to biggest." Patterns, sequence, and order work together in art and design. The mathart experiences in chapter three range from making simple patterns, copying patterns, and creating patterns, to extending patterns into sequences and order.

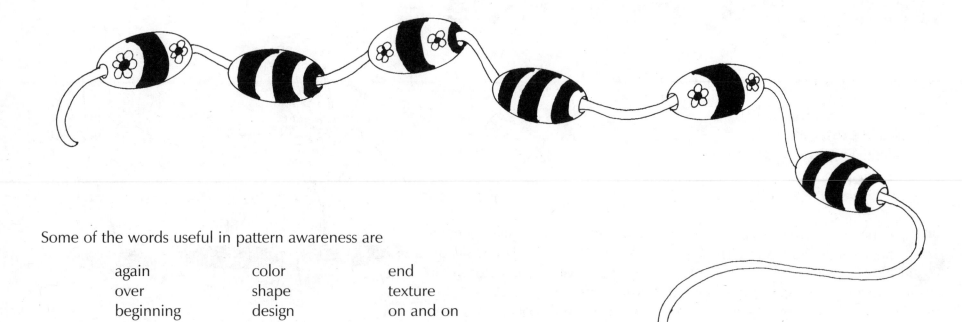

Some of the words useful in pattern awareness are

again	color	end
over	shape	texture
beginning	design	on and on
repeat	start to finish	over and under

Crepe Paper Pattern

Patterns of bright watercolor markings are created with crepe paper rolled into a painting tool and used as a paintbrush.

Materials

✓ crepe paper in a variety of colors, party-roll style
✓ tape (optional)
✓ cup of water
✓ paper
✓ aluminum foil or latex gloves (optional)

Process

1. Roll a piece of crepe paper into a tube the size of a crayon. Tape the roll, if desired.
2. Dip the tip of the tube into the cup of water.
3. Brush the wet crepe paper tube across the paper, painting color onto the paper.
4. Select a new color, and continue dipping and painting, creating a colorful pattern.
   Hint: If desired, wrap foil around the crepe paper where it will be held to protect fingers from staining or wear latex gloves.

Variations

■ Roll several layers of colors together to make a tube that will mix colors as you go. Sometimes brown is the resulting color!
■ Paint with crepe paper tubes on fabric, wood, or absorbent paper such as paper towels or white tissue paper.

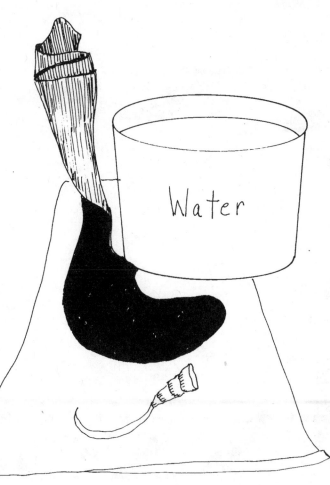

45

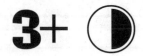

**patterns
clay**

Patterned Clay Snakes

S nakes of clay are the most common, natural outcomes of clay exploration for young children. Use clay in a variety of colors to allow for exploring patterns.

Materials

✓ 2 or more colors of nontoxic polymer modeling clay, such as Fimo
✓ oven preheated to 275°F
✓ glass baking pan

Process

1. Pinch off a marble-size ball of clay, one for each color in the patterned snake. Two to four colors work well.
2. Roll each ball into a rope or long snake.
3. Twist the ropes together.
4. Now roll the mixed ropes into a new, smooth colorful snake.
5. Flatten one end of the snake for a head. Add little eyes and a tongue, if desired.
6. Bake for about 10 minutes on a glass pan in the oven.
7. Cool completely. Remove the snake carefully; some sticking may occur and is to be expected.

Variations

■ Add spots to the snake by pressing balls into little circles. Press the circles onto the rope, and then roll the rope to smooth the spots into the rope.
■ Flat Snakes can be made by rolling the snake with a rolling pin. Artists find this extremely funny.

No Bake Beads

 (caution) ⬛ 🖐 🕐 **3+**

Artists focus on making patterns of colors or shapes with beads they have created.

Materials
- ✓ elastic string, cut long enough to make a necklace to slip over the head
- ✓ block of styrofoam or ball of play dough
- ✓ toothpicks

Process
1. Pinch a bit of dough from a ball of colored dough. Roll the piece into a bead shape (round, cube, cylinder, cone).
2. Poke a hole in the bead with a toothpick.
3. Leave the bead on the toothpick to dry, sticking the toothpick with the bead into a block of styrofoam or a ball of play dough. Turn beads occasionally so they do not stick to the toothpicks.
4. Dry the beads until hard, usually 1 or 2 days. Speed dry beads in the oven at 200°F for 1 hour.
5. When dry, sort the beads into colors. String a pattern of beads according to their colors on the elastic string.
6. Tie the ends of the elastic string together to form a necklace. Slip over the head and wear or give as a gift.

Variations
- Make bead strings for a garland to drape around a room or wind around a Christmas tree.
- Make a bracelet, headband, or sash instead of a necklace.

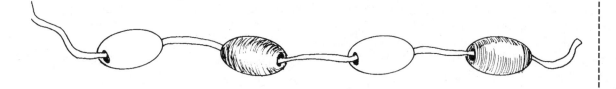

Dough Recipe

1 cup salt
1 cup water
1/2 cup cold water
1 cup cornstarch
spoon, bowl, pan, and stove

Mix 1 cup salt and 1 cup water. Boil in a pan, with adult help. Stir 1/2 cup cold water into 1 cup cornstarch in a bowl. Add the cornstarch mixture to the boiling water and stir. Cook over low heat, stirring until like pie dough. Remove and turn onto a board. When cool, knead until smooth. For a colored dough, add food coloring to a ball of dough, kneading the color into it. Make several balls of dough, making each ball a different color.

47

Geometric Wrapping Illusion

By cutting and pasting striped wrapping paper in a simple pattern, an illusionary collage is created.

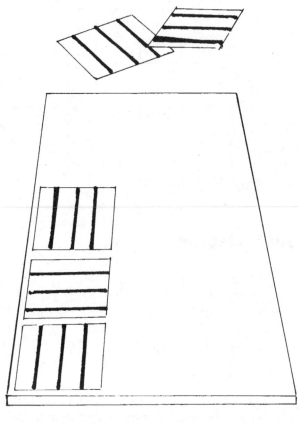

Materials
✓ striped or lined wrapping paper
✓ scissors
✓ paste or white glue
✓ cardboard, matte board, or sheet of paper for base, about 12" x 24"

Process
1. With adult help precut striped or lined wrapping paper into 4" squares. Place on the table.
2. Paste or glue the first square in the uppermost corner of the base paper. Notice which way the stripes are going: side to side, or up and down.
3. Next, paste another square of wrapping paper next to the first one, turning the stripes a different direction this time.
4. Paste the third square next to the second and turn the stripes again.
5. Continue pasting squares to cover the entire base paper, keeping the stripes going in changing directions.
6. When the entire sheet is full, post the design on the wall. Stand across the room and look at the optical illusion.

Variations
- Allow very young children to explore, placing the squares in a design of their choosing.
- Fold a paper for the base of the design in equal squares of any size. Unfold. Cut wrapping paper with lines or stripes into squares that will fit into the folded squares of the base paper. Paste the squares of wrapping paper in the folded squares of the base paper. Turn the squares this way and that to achieve an optical illusion.
- Use wrapping paper from two different, contrasting paper designs to produce a strong optical effect.

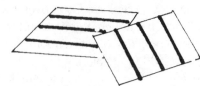

Sticky-Dot Illusion

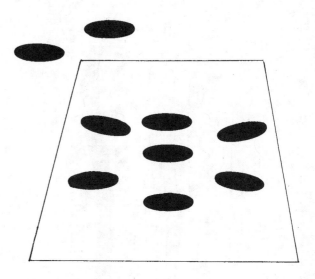

S ticky-dots create an optical geometric illusion when placed in a pattern on a paper of contrasting color. Look at a color wheel to see which colors are opposites and, therefore, most contrasting.

Materials
✓ sticky-dots, one color
✓ contrasting color of base paper, about 8" x 10"

Process
1. Choose a color of sticky-dots and then a contrasting color of paper. For example, yellow dots on purple paper work as an effective illusionary combination.
2. Stick a yellow dot on the purple paper. Then another. Then another and another and another. Try to leave purple paper showing between the dots.
3. When the paper is well filled with dots, stand back and look at the design. For more optical fun, stare at the design for a little while, and then stare at a white wall. See the dots?

Variations
■ Use two sizes of dots of the same color on a contrasting paper. Try to make patterns with the large and small dots for an optically stimulating experience.
■ Cut construction paper or colorful sticky-backed paper into squares, circles, and other shapes from several colors. Create a collage on a contrasting color of base paper. Incorporate patterns for wonderfully weird optical results.

3+ ⏻ ✋

Pretty Ribbon Wall Hanging

Ribbons glued to a flat piece of larger fabric create a design with a pattern.

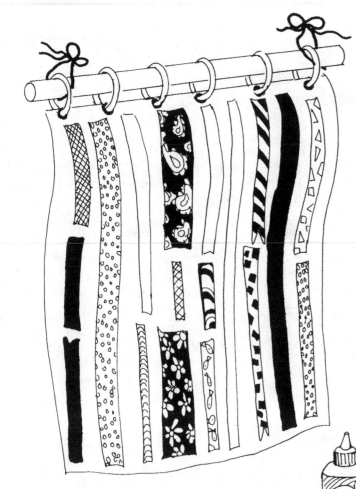

Materials
✓ ribbons or fabric strips cut to manageable lengths
✓ scissors
✓ fabric glue or craft glue
✓ large piece of heavy plain fabric in any size or shape
✓ wooden dowel, old mop handle, or other stick
✓ cafe curtain rings or shower curtain rings
✓ hole punch

Process
1. Glue a ribbon down flat on the fabric using the fabric glue.
2. Place another ribbon piece beside it and glue into place.
3. Continue gluing ribbon on the fabric, repeating ribbon colors to create a pattern. Dry completely.
4. When dry, punch holes evenly spaced across one edge of the fabric. Make as many holes as you have curtain rings. If the hole punch won't work, snip little holes with the scissors instead.
5. Insert the curtain rings, one in each hole. Slide the curtain rings over the dowel.
6. With leftover ribbon or fabric, tie the first ring and the last ring to the dowel to keep the rings from sliding off the dowel.
7. Hang on the wall to enjoy or use to decorate a window.

Variations
■ Bend, curl, or snip the ribbon for a different look.
■ Sew a simple casing down one side of the fabric, slide a dowel into it, and create a simple flag.

Poke-It-Card Pattern

There are many patterns in this mathart activity, from the patterns of beads used to the patterns of the holes poked in the card.

Materials
✓ poster board or lightweight cardboard
✓ colorful yarn or string
✓ bits of paper, beads, and other odds and ends with holes
✓ paper punch
✓ scissors
✓ tape
   Note: Use caution with young children who still put small objects in their mouths.

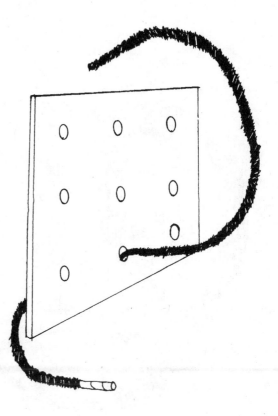

Process
1. Cut poster board into cards about 5" x 5".
2. Punch holes in the card in a random or planned pattern. If more holes are desired where the paper punch cannot reach, use the tips of a pair of scissors to push through more holes (with adult assistance, if needed).
3. Tape or tie one end of the yarn to the back of the card. Wrap the other end of the yarn with a piece of tape to form a "needle."
4. The artist laces the yarn in and out of the holes, adding extra texture and design with beads, paper bits punched with holes for stringing, or other odds and ends that have holes for stringing. If items do not have holes, add some with the paper punch.
5. When the sewing yarn runs out, tape it to the back of the card. Then add more yarn and continue lacing and adding decorative items.
6. Cards can be worn about the neck for display, hung on the wall, or strung together like a large decorative garland.

Variations
■ Join several cards together on a clothesline or on one long piece of yarn like a garland.
■ For a bright card background, before punching the holes in the cardboard, paint with marbling designs, colorful patterns, or glue on geometric shapes.

51

Pipe Cleaner Garland

Pipe cleaners are a simple, familiar mathart material with many uses. One of them is placing loops of color in a pattern for a garland.

Materials
✓ pipe cleaners or chenille stems in a variety of colors

Process
1. Place pipe cleaners in a pile. Sort the pipe cleaners by color into separate piles.
2. Select a color and bend the pipe cleaner to form a loop. Twist the ends together to close the loop.
3. Select another color pipe cleaner and bend it around the first one to form another loop. Twist the ends together. (This will resemble a chain made from paper, but can be formed into shapes other than circles, such as squares, triangles, and abstract shapes.)
4. Create a pattern of repeated colors of pipe cleaners.

Variations
■ Twist pipe cleaners around a rope or dowel rod in a sequential order.
■ Push pipe cleaners into a long coil of modeling clay or into a piece of styrofoam in a sequential arrangement.
■ Substitute colored wire for the pipe cleaners.

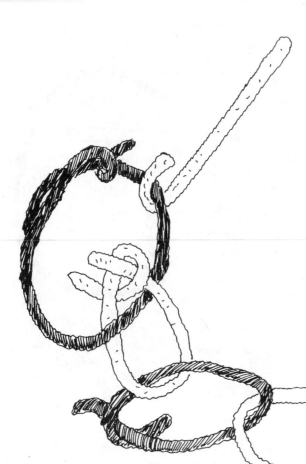

String Pattern Construction

3+

A board with nails becomes a versatile, changeable base for designs allowing many different experiences with color, design, and pattern unique to each artist.

Materials
✓ flat piece of wood, about 1" thick
✓ colorful string, rubber bands, embroidery floss, or heavy thread
✓ hammer
✓ nails (about 30)

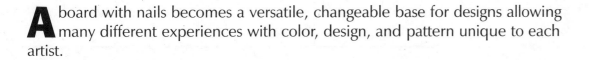

Process
1. First, think about hammering nails into the flat piece of wood in rows, a circle shape, or any other pattern.
2. Then, with adult help, hammer about 30 nails into the wood in the thought-out pattern. (Be careful that nails do not poke through the wood into the work surface.) Hammer the nails so that about 1" of each nail is visible.
3. Next, take a piece of colored string and wrap the end several times around a nail. Tie to secure if necessary.
4. Pull the string tight over to another nail and wrap it once or twice around the second nail.
5. Pull the string to another and another nail, wrapping string around different nails to create a pattern. Change colors of string at any time, if desired. (Rubber bands work well, but be careful. They can snap.)
6. The string can be removed after a period of time and the board used again by someone new.

Variations
■ Allow very young children decide on the design, and an adult can hammer the nails into the wood.
■ Push map pins or other push-pins into a ceiling tile or piece of thick styrofoam. Wrap and wind colorful string or embroidery floss from pin to pin.
■ Form a shape or picture (like "follow the dot") with the nails or pins such as a ship, flower, animal, truck. Use colors as desired.

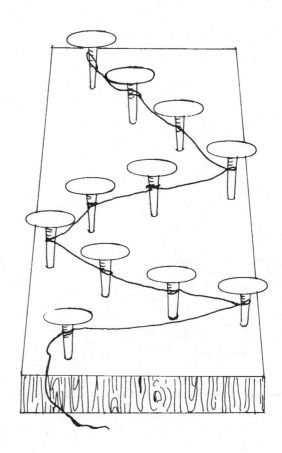

53

**patterns
construction**

Stretchy Pattern Board

Give an artist a hammer and nails, add the snap, color, and versatility of rubber bands, and creating patterns becomes inspired and simple to do.

Materials

✓ square of flat wood, about 12" x 12" and about 1" thick
✓ large head nails, at least 16
✓ rubber bands in a variety of colors

Process

1. With adult help hammer four nails down each side of the wood square, evenly spaced and sticking out from the wood about 1/2" to 1". (Be careful not to nail the board to the work surface.) More nails may be added on each of the four sides if desired, but each side should have an even number.
2. Sort rubber bands by color into piles on the table.
3. Think about a pattern of colors, such as
   Red, blue; red, blue; repeat
   Red, blue, yellow, yellow; red, blue, yellow, yellow; repeat
   Red, blue horizontally; yellow, green vertically; repeat
   (Any pattern is acceptable. Very simple ones are nice for beginning. More colors can be added later, if desired.)
4. Select a color. Place the first color rubber band over one nail and stretch it across the board to the opposite nail.
5. Select a second color. Place the second color rubber band over another nail and stretch it across the board to the opposite nail.
6. Continue stretching rubber bands over nails until the pattern board is filled as desired.
7. Rubber bands may be removed for new creations or added to for extended creations.

Variation

■ The board itself can also be changed or designed, such as:
   Paint the board before nailing.
   Cover the board with wrapping paper, foil, or other paper.
   Paint the sections between rubber bands after nailing.
   Stain the board with wet art tissue paper or commercial stain.

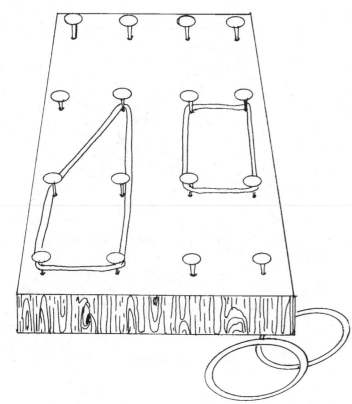

Pattern Resist

Drawing a pattern with crayon takes on new life when a paint wash of thinned tempera paint is brushed over the crayon pattern design.

Materials

✓ crayons, markers, pencils, pens
✓ paper
✓ tempera paint wash in a jar (A wash is a very thin, watery mixture of tempera paint and water. Thinned watercolor paint or food coloring also work.)
✓ soft paintbrush
✓ scissors
✓ large sheets of colored paper

Process

1. Use crayons to make a pattern of stripes on paper. Any pattern will do, such as red, red, blue, yellow; repeat. Each artist can design any pattern desired.
2. Repeat the pattern until the paper is filled with patterns of stripes. When a pattern is repeated, it is called a sequence of patterns.
3. Next, wash over the crayon patterns with a thin mixture of tempera paint and water. Use a soft brush filled with the wash.
4. Watch the crayon patterns resist the paint. Then dry briefly.
5. Use scissors to cut the Pattern Resist into a large shape, such as a circle, cloud, flower, T-shirt, or any abstract shape. Make additional Pattern Resists.
6. Pattern Resists are effective glued on a large sheet of colored paper for a contrasting or a matching background.

Tempera Water Mixture

Variations

■ For older children number the crayons or markers with number labels and make a Pattern Resist according to the number on the crayon, such as a

     1, 2, 3 pattern
     1, 5, 2 pattern
     5, 5, 5, 1, 2 pattern

■ Place each color of markers in a separate container. Then, make a Pattern Resist by selecting and drawing with colors from the cups in the order of the cup placement on the table.

**sequence
drawing**

Connect the Dots Design

The results of connecting dots in a sequence are never the same from one experience to the next. Although the grids start out the same, the results are varied.

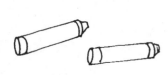

Materials

✓ paper with predrawn dots (or sticky-dots)
✓ markers
✓ crayons
✓ paper scraps, white glue, scissors, yarn (optional)

Process

1. An adult prepares the paper with dots. Draw or stick dots in an even pattern on the paper as shown in the illustrations. (A photocopy machine is helpful when preparing more than two or three for a group.)
2. The artist connects the dots with colored markers or crayons. As few or as many dots can be connected as desired. Some can be skipped too.
3. For extra color and design, color in the shapes formed by connecting the dots, or cut bits of paper scraps and glue them into the spaces formed between the lines and dots. Lines may also be outlined with yarn glued over the lines.

Variations

■ Create a Connect the Dots design with yarn glued on the paper.
■ Create a Connect the Nails design with nails hammered in a square board and wrap yarn from one nail to the next.
■ Sew colored yarn from one punched (or poked) hole in a piece of matte board or a styrofoam tray to another hole. Holes could be numbered to increase the difficulty of any of the above projects.

Good Old Paper Chains

Making paper chains is an activity that is remarkably popular with children and incorporates the concept of pattern and sequence.

Materials

✓ colored or white paper, cut into strips (any width or length)
✓ pencils, crayons, markers, or paints and brushes
✓ stapler or tape

Process

1. Draw or paint on strips of paper with designs or pictures. (Painting and drawing could also be done before the strips are cut. Dry, then cut. Adult help may be needed.)
2. Stack the strips of paper into piles according to similar colors, pictures, or designs.
3. Staple or tape the ends of one strip of paper together into a loop.
4. The loop can be pinched, or the loop can be round. (See illustration.)
5. Slip another paper strip through the center of the first loop, or link, of the chain and staple or tape the ends to form another link of the paper chain.
6. Create a pattern by repeating colors or decorations until the paper chain is any length desired.

Variations

■ For "fat" chains, strips of paper can be about 2" to 3" wide and 6" to 8" long. For slim chains, strips can be about 1" wide and 8" long.
■ Chains can decorate a room with a holiday or seasonal theme, such as pastels for spring, blue and white for winter, red and green for Christmas.
■ Chains can keep track of days going by until a special event, such as How many days until my birthday? Make a chain with the number of links until the birthday. Tear one off each day and see the special day get closer and closer. Links can be numbered, counting backward to one, if desired.

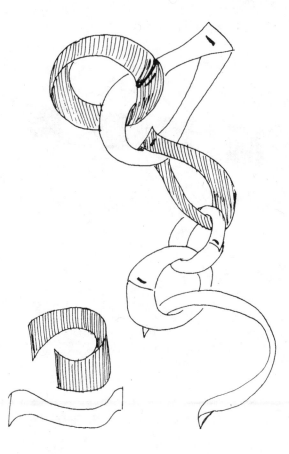

57

3+

**sequence
construction**

Sequence-a-Pattern Colored Blocks

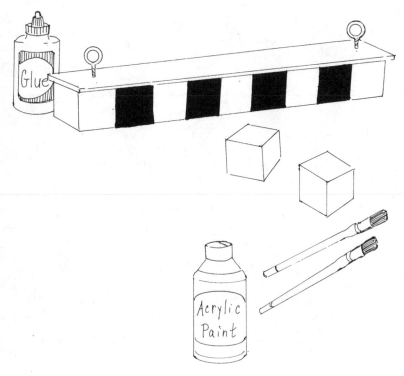

Aligning homemade painted blocks creates a sequence of colors, shapes, or designs. When the same sequence is repeated, this sequence becomes a pattern.

Materials

✓ wooden blocks, commercial or homemade
✓ acrylic paint and brushes
✓ newspaper
✓ white glue
✓ narrow board to use as a base for gluing
✓ screw in eye hooks, at least 2 (optional)
✓ yarn, string, or wire (optional)

Process

1. Paint the wooden blocks with nontoxic acrylic paint in any style, using colors and brush strokes freely. Cover completely or partially.
2. Let the blocks dry on newspaper overnight. Clean brushes and work area while waiting.
3. When the blocks are dry, align the painted blocks to create a sequence of colors, shapes, or designs. Then, repeat this sequence. This makes a pattern of repeated sequences.
4. Glue this pattern of sequenced blocks onto the longer narrow board. Dry overnight.
5. Screw in one eye hook at the right hand top edge of the board, and another eye hook at the other end, at the top edge of the board. Now wire, string, or yarn can be strung through the eye hooks so the Colored Block Construction can be hung on the wall, in a window, or high up in a doorway.

Variations

■ Use other materials cut into shapes for forming a sequence and then a pattern that can be glued to a wooden board, such as
> art tissue scraps, used deck of cards, bottle caps, collage items,
> checkers and toy parts, leaves from outdoors
■ No paint? Use food coloring or fabric dye with brushes.

58

Ordered Tube Hanging

Different sizes or colors of paper towel cardboard tubes are a free and easy math manipulative. Tubes can be sorted by color, by size, or by other attributes, then the tubes are strung on a cord and draped around the room like a garland to show the ordering.

Materials

✓ toilet paper and paper towel tubes
✓ scissors
✓ tempera paints in many colors
✓ paintbrushes
✓ cord or twine
✓ newspaper to cover work space

Process

1. Cut paper tubes into different lengths.
2. Paint the paper tubes with tempera paint.
3. Stand on end to dry.
4. Place paper tubes in order by one of the following:
   bright to dull colors
   primary to secondary colors
   plain to patterned designs
   short to tall
5. String cord or twine through each tube like a garland, keeping the tubes in the order selected.
6. Hang to display or for decoration.

Variations

■ Cut paper tubes into narrow rings using scissors and string on yarn for a necklace, bracelet, or a Hawaiian lei.
■ Reuse flexible plastic tubing or pipe cut into rings and stack the rings on wooden doweling. Use permanent markers to decorate and color the rings.

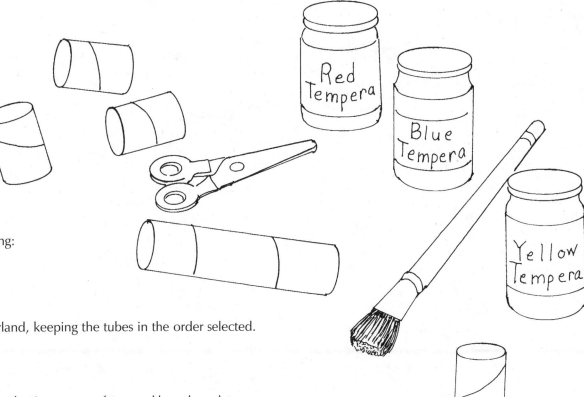

**order
collage**

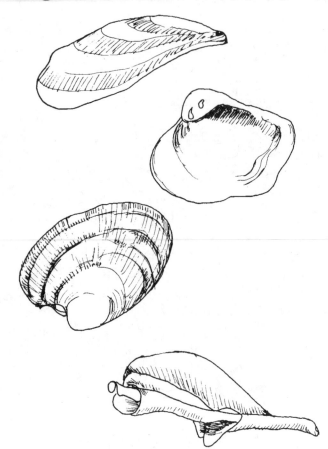

Seashell Arrangement

The artist places shells in order by size, color, texture, or markings. Adding a coat of clear paint enhances the natural colors and designs of the shells.

Materials
✓ assorted seashells
✓ white glue
✓ hot glue-gun (optional, with close adult supervision only)
✓ piece of smooth wood, masonite, or heavy cardboard
✓ clear hobby paint, brushes (optional)

Process
1. Put all seashells into a pile on a table or tray.
2. Place seashells in order in one of the following ways:
   - large to small
   - dark to light colors
   - flat to rounded
   - smooth to textured
   - plain to decorative
3. Place one of the orders of shells in a design or arrangement on wood, masonite, or heavy cardboard.
4. Glue into place.
5. Dry overnight or longer.
6. When dry, paint if desired, or cover with a coat of clear hobby paint to enhance the natural colors of the shells.

Variation
■ An adult can carefully drill a small hole in each seashell with a hand drill, and the artist can string the seashells to create an ordered mobile, garland, or necklace.

Leaf Arrangement

When the leaves are placed in order according to a design, the leaf arrangement takes on a balance and pattern.

Materials

- ✓ leaves in assorted shapes and sizes
- ✓ newsprint to cover work area
- ✓ white glue
- ✓ poster board or matte board
- ✓ crayons and markers
- ✓ clear plastic wrap
- ✓ tape

Process

1. Spread leaves in a pile on a large sheet of newsprint.
2. Put leaves in order using one of the following:

   smooth to rough edged

   single to many points

   small to large

   plain to multicolored (if autumn leaves are used)
3. Glue an arrangement of ordered leaves to the poster board.
4. Use crayons and markers to further decorate the leaf arrangement.
5. To save and protect the work stretch a piece of clear plastic wrap over the arrangement, taping it to the back of the poster board.

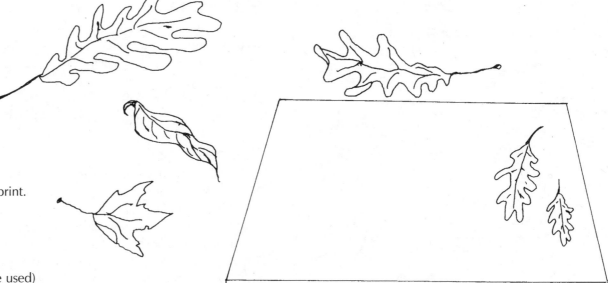

Variations

- ■ Place leaves between layers of wax paper, cover with newspaper, and iron with a warm iron. The leaves will be sealed between the sheets of wax paper. Display the creations in a window to see the "stained glass" effect and silhouettes of the leaves.
- ■ Cut paper leaf shapes from wallpaper, wrapping paper, old posters, or other papers. Follow the same directions for paper leaves as for real leaves above.

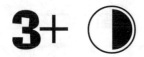

3+

order
craft

Colored Sand Glass

Placing the jars of colored sand in an order devised by the artist helps her focus on sorting by likes and differences and degrees in between.

Materials
✓ clean sand
✓ food coloring or powdered tempera paint, in several colors
✓ bowls for mixing, 1 for each color
✓ stirring sticks
✓ spoon, scoop, or small shovel
✓ transparent jars in large, medium, and small sizes (with lids)

Process
1. Pour some sand into the mixing bowl.
2. Add a few drops of food coloring or powdered tempera to color the sand. Stir with the stick to blend color evenly.
3. Mix more sand in a new color. Make as many colors as you wish.
4. Spoon, scoop, or shovel colored sand into jars.
5. Create and order the colorful jars by placing them into sets according to size or color.
6. Line up the jars on a shelf or windowsill to enjoy.

Variations
■ Pour colored sand in styrofoam trays or box lids. Next, paint one side of a 3" x 5" card with glue. (Cards may be cut into different shapes.) Press the glue side of the card into the colored sand, remove, and dry. Create cards for each color of sand. Use the cards to sort and put in order by color or shape, or to glue onto a larger poster board in a pattern.
■ Save spools or small blocks of wood. Dip one end in glue and then into colored sand. Dry completely. When dry, sort and order the colorful spools or blocks on a larger scrap of wood. Glue them in place.

PART 2

I'm On My Way...
Exploring Spatial
Relationships

CHAPTER 4

Near, Far, Up, Down

Math concepts explored in this chapter

Proximity
Direction
Opposites
Balance
Symmetry

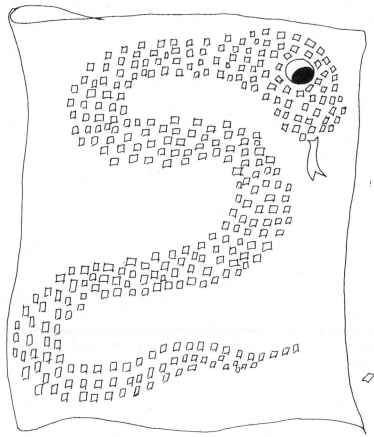

Young children begin exploring math by exploring their own environments and interacting with materials and objects around them. The concept of proximity builds an understanding of basic areas of mathematics, such as

✓ measuring
✓ geometry
✓ putting things in order
✓ understanding shapes
✓ putting things in sequence

Proximity is the concept of an item in space and its position, direction, and relationship in distance to other objects. Activities to learn about proximity and direction are numerous and can last over most of the young learners' early education. Repeating activities with different materials and objects helps reinforce the experiences.

Part of exploring the concept of opposites is learning how shapes relate to each other, such as right and left, top and bottom, high and low. Young children will learn the names of the shapes while working with them. They will also explore the concept of balance with mathart activities that allow them to discover the relationship of one object to another. Symmetry means that the two sides of a design are exact mirror images of each other, like the wings of a butterfly.

Some of the words young learners can use are:

up	outside
down	enclosed
near	stop
far	go
next to	left
between	right
front	side by side
back	high
touching	low
leave a space	over
on the line	under
connect	through
on top of	in the middle of
close	background
far away	foreground
inside	

Exploring Spatial Relationships

Line and Dot Mural

First the artist dabs dots all over a large sheet of paper. When the dots have dried, the artist adds lines between, over, around, and near the dots, creating a winding, bright mathart experience.

Materials

✓ very large paper or cardboard
✓ masking tape
✓ paints and brushes
✓ markers

Process

1. Tape the large sheet of paper or cardboard to the wall at child's height.
2. Paint and dab dots freely all over the paper or cardboard.
3. Draw lines freely above, below, over, around, and between the painted dots.
4. Dry completely.

Variations

■ Add further decoration to the mural with stickers, yarn, glue, paper shapes.
■ Create a Line and Dot Mural using a chalk board and colored chalks.
■ Create an outdoors mural by taping a large sheet of paper on a fence.
■ Further decorate with items collected outside, such as
  pinecones
  seeds
  blossoms
  pine needles
  pebbles
  leaves

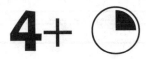

4+

**proximity
painting**

Discovery Watercolor

The use of watercolors is a refreshing technique to explore the proximity of paint colors to each other, the relationships and combinations of colors as paints touch, merge, and blend together.

Materials
✓ watercolors in red, blue, violet, yellow, green, orange
✓ water in large plastic container
✓ paintbrushes
✓ sheet of heavy white paper
✓ black felt marker

Process
1. Fill the paintbrush with one color, dripping and very wet.
2. Paint on a sheet of heavy white paper with the dripping paint. Make a puddle of color or a wiggly shape. Rinse the brush.
3. Paint another color right next to the first color. See the two colors touch and blend, their proximity revealed. Rinse the brush.
4. Keep adding areas of bright watercolors. Leave some areas white too. Dry the painting overnight.
5. Outline every puddle of paint with the black felt maarker, especially wherever the paints change colors.
6. Stand back and look for surprise shapes in the painting. There may be a face, a strange creature, a monster, or a beautiful bird.

Variations
■ Cut out the shapes and glue them on another piece of paper.
■ Cut out the shapes and sandwich them between sheets of clear self-adhesive paper.
■ Enhance the design with glitter-glue or other art materials on the outlined areas.
■ Before painting, draw with white crayon on the paper to add a crayon resist to the Discovery Watercolor.

Sticky Back Stamps

In this variation of print-making, the young learner explores the relationship of prints that are crowded together, spread apart, or overlapping each other.

Materials
✓ roll of insulation tape, peel-off variety from a hardware store
✓ small wooden blocks
✓ scissors
✓ hole punch
✓ ink pads, different colors or multicolored
✓ newspaper
✓ paper

Process
1. Cut a piece of the tape.
2. Punch holes in the piece of tape and stick the holes directly to the wooden block. Cut other shapes from the tape and stick those to the wooden block too. This is the stamp block.
3. Press the stamp block on an ink pad, dabbing and pressing it a few times to get an even coating of ink.
4. Press the stamp on the paper. Press firmly but gently and try not to wiggle. Smashing the stamp on the paper doesn't make it work better.
5. Before changing to a new color of ink, press the stamp on the newspaper several times until the old color is gone.

(Continued on next page)

Face Stamp

Fade Away

69

Checkerboard

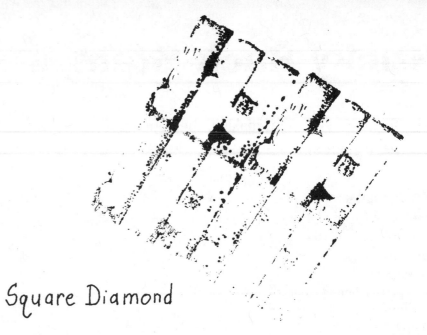

Square Diamond

Brick Building

Variations

Experiment with pattern ideas or make up unique, individually designed patterns.

- **Face Stamp**: Create a face using hole punches from the sticky tape. After the face is stamped on the paper, add details with a marker, such as hair, jewelry, body, eyelashes, lips.

- **Fade Away**: Stamp the design over and over, overlapping the designs across the paper. The stamps will become fainter and fainter as the ink is used up.

- **Square Diamond**: Make a diamond from squares. Stamp the block four times, four sides touching each other. Rotate the block each time a stamp is pressed.

- **Brick Building**: Stamp a design over and over in a straight row. Next, make another row on top of the first but off center a bit, just like the bricks in a building.

- **Checkerboard**: Stamp a design in steps, with corners touching. Go back and add more stamps, similar to a checker board.

70

River Pebble Display

When small stones are placed in a defined area, young learners explore the concept of proximity, an early introduction to the mathematical concept of geometry.

4+

proximity sculpture

Materials

✓ smooth round river pebbles of different sizes (or landscape pebbles)
✓ 1 larger pebble wrapped in foil (or painted gold)
✓ modeling clay
✓ tempera paints or markers

Process

1. Push modeling clay into the shoe box, covering the bottom and inside walls.
2. Place the shiny rock in the box. Add other pebbles to the box.
3. Create arrangements of pebbles in relation to the shiny rock, using some or all of the following words:

   between, beside, inside, under, on top of,
   above, through, near, outside
4. Push the pebbles and shiny rock deeper into the modeling clay to form a permanent display of one of the arrangements.
5. Using tempera paint or markers, create designs and colors on the rocks.

Variations

- Create a landscape with a variety of colors of modeling clay to indicate rivers and land. Add collage items to complete the design. Sticks could be used for trees, bits of paper for houses, a bottle cap for a table, and so on. Work on a cookie sheet or piece of heavy cardboard.
- Design a map with pebbles, modeling clay, and small figurines.
- Experiment with a map of a real location, such as a walk around the block. Work on a cookie sheet or piece of heavy cardboard.

71

**proximity
sculpture**

Paper Cup Mobile

Bright paper cups dangling on various lengths of string combine a sculptural mathart experience while exploring proximity.

Materials
✓ paper cups
✓ markers
✓ colored glue or white glue
✓ glitter
✓ art tissue
✓ scissors
✓ string
✓ paper clips
✓ dowel rod or clothes hanger

Process
1. Decorate plain paper cups with markers. Next, add colored glue, glitter, and bits of art tissue to the cups. (Use white glue if colored glue is not available.)
2. With adult help, punch a small hole in the bottom of each cup.
3. Cut a length of string and tie a paper clip on one end.
4. Push the string through the hole from the inside of the cup out. Then, pull through until the paper clip rests against the bottom inside of the cup.
5. Hang the decorated cup from a hanger or dowel rod. Tape or tie the string to the hanger.
6. Hang more decorated cups at different lengths and distances from each other on the hanger or rod.
7. Add another piece of string to the hanger or rod and hang the entire mobile from the ceiling or a high point in the room.

Variation
■ Instead of paper cups, decorate any of the following items for a mobile, such as tag board shapes, small toy pieces, magazine pictures glued to paper circles, printed paper shapes, jar lids, bottle caps

Stacking Balls Sculpture

  4+

The young learner pushes, pulls, squeezes, and stacks balls of clay while exploring proximity and making a freeform sculpture.

Materials

✓ modeling clay or play dough in assorted colors (see page 88 for a good play dough recipe or use your own favorite)
✓ tools for clay modeling, such as
     plastic knife, small toy parts, block of wood,
     rolling pin, cookie cutters, toothpicks

Process

1. Shape and roll pinches of clay or playdough into balls of various sizes.
2. Stack the colorful balls and form them into a three-dimensional shape (one that rises from the table rather than remaining flat).
3. Experiment with clay tools and make other shapes. Stack these into a different sculpture or add to the Stacking Balls Sculpture.

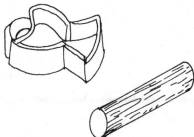

Hints

■ The sculpture will be temporary because modeling clay will not harden, and play dough will eventually dry out and crumble.
■ To reuse clay or play dough, take the sculpture apart when ready, and use the clay or dough again later.
■ Play dough stores well in an airtight container.
■ Modeling clay lasts a long time without any particular storage.

Variations

■ Use cookie cutter shapes and stack them into a three-dimensional form.
■ Stack (and glue or tape) any of the following into a sculpture:
     milk cartons, building toys, blocks, spools, boxes,
     soup cans, paper cups, yogurt cups

73

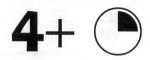

**proximity
collage**

Shiny Curly Cues

This project gives the artist a beginning experience of how pieces of aluminum foil relate to each other when taped to the matte board.

Materials
✓ aluminum foil
✓ matte board
✓ transparent tape
✓ scissors
✓ metallic stickers

Process
1. Cut or tear aluminum foil into strips.
2. Tape the strips in different ways on the matte board. Bend and twist the strips to add design.
3. During the creating, note strips that are near, touching, above, below, and between other strips.
4. Stick metallic stickers to the design to add additional sparkle.

Variations
■ Use metallic gift wrap paper, metallic ribbon, metallic candy wrappers, and metallic tape for an alternate sparkly, shiny artwork.
■ Use cut foil shapes instead of tearing the foil into strips.
■ Use construction paper scraps instead of foil for Colorful Curly Cues.

Mosaic Mat

4+

The artist presses bright colored paper squares to a sticky sheet of clear self-adhesive paper. The mathart focus is to explore the placement of colored paper squares in relationship one to another.

Materials

- ✓ self-adhesive paper (black or any color or pattern), about 10" x 15" (the approximate size of a place mat)
- ✓ another sheet of clear self-adhesive paper about the same size or slightly larger
- ✓ tape
- ✓ scissors
- ✓ construction paper cut in 1" squares in several colors

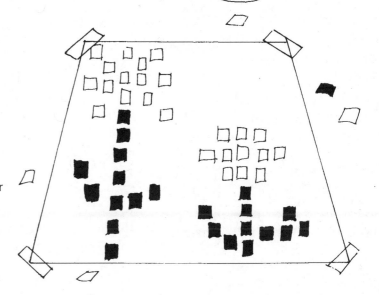

Process

1. Peel the covering from the self-adhesive paper. Place it sticky side up on the table.
2. Tape the corners to the table to help keep the mat in place.
3. Create a mosaic design by sticking squares of construction paper to the self-adhesive paper, leaving small spaces between squares. Squares may also be cut into other shapes to add to the design.
4. When the mat is covered with squares, peel the backing from the clear self-adhesive paper. Note: Adult help will be needed for steps 4 and 5.
5. Stick the clear paper over the top of the mosaic design. Expect wrinkles and pleats.
6. Trim the edges straight or wiggly with the scissors.
7. The Mosaic Mat can be used as a place mat that can be wiped clean with a damp sponge or as table art, wall art, or any other decoration.

Variation

- Create a mat with art tissue squares, torn or cut.

75

4+ ◑

**direction
drawing**

Sidewalk Shapes

The young artist creates a myriad of colorful shapes with chalk on a sidewalk or playground area and then jumps, walks, and tiptoes through the shapes.

Materials
✓ large sidewalk chalk
✓ sidewalk or concrete play area

Process
1. Draw shapes on a sidewalk or concrete play area.
2. Draw shapes near, far, between, and beside other shapes.
3. When shapes are drawn and completed, the artist walks, skips, or jumps over, around, and between the chalk shapes.

Variations
■ Hose down a sidewalk with water and then draw with chalk on the wet sidewalk for chalk that acts more like paint. Use a sponge to blend colors together.
■ Draw on a large sheet of butcher paper taped to the floor. Walk or move on the drawing in socks. Colors can be blended with socks. Keep in mind that the color in chalky-socks may not wash out completely, but they are very pretty!

Left Side Sunshine, Right Side Rainbow

The young artist paints hands, face, or forearm with makeup, making distinctive designs on the left side and different designs on the right side.

Materials
✓ clown face makeup or Halloween face paints
✓ cold cream and soft paper towels
✓ paintbrushes, makeup brushes, cotton swabs

Process
1. Indicate to the child which is the left and right side of the body.
2. Place a yellow dot on the child's left cheek, hand, or forearm; place a red dot on his right cheek, hand, or forearm.
3. The artist paints a sunshine or other yellow design on his left cheek, hand, or forearm.
4. The artist paints a rainbow or other design with red on his right cheek, hand, or forearm.
5. Other designs may be added to the left or right. Use the words left and right while the artist is painting.
6. To clean the paint or makeup gently and thoroughly from skin, wipe away the designs with cold cream and soft paper towels. Wipe gently.

Variations
■ Draw other designs or pictures indicating left and right side of the body on knees, toes, feet, legs.
■ Make little flags, bracelets, decorated shoelaces, or other items for the child to wear, yellow for left and red for right.
■ Create yellow and red footprints from clear self-adhesive paper and stick them to the carpet. The child hops with left or right feet on the yellow or red footprints. Remove the footprints the same day.

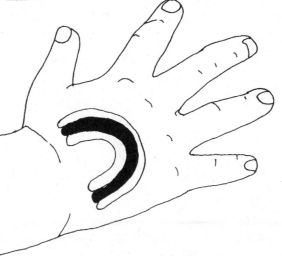

77

4+ ◑ ✋ Handy Hide and Find

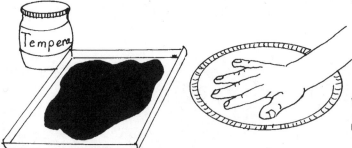

Creating fingerpaint handprints on paper plates becomes a math activity when the young child must find the prints she has made displayed among many others, an experience with direction.

Materials
✓ tempera paint or fingerpaint in a flat dish or tray
✓ paper plates
✓ masking tape
✓ large poster board or craft paper
✓ markers
✓ chalk board and chalk
✓ bucket filled with soapy water
✓ old towels for drying hands

Process
1. Dip the palm of the hand in the paint.
2. Press painted hand on the paper plate to make a handprint.
3. Make as many handprint plates in as many colors as desired.
4. Let plates dry. Wash and dry hands.
5. Place a loop of masking tape on the back of the paper plate.
6. Stick handprint plates around a room or outside.
7. Find handprints like a treasure hunt. Try to identify the owners of each print.
8. Collect the handprint plates and create one of the following activities:
      Cover one wall with all the handprints.
      Cover a table with all the handprints.
      Cover a door with all the handprints.
      Create a mural or border of handprint plates.

Variation
■ Cut the handprints from the plates and use for other ideas, such as
      tape to straws to resemble flowers
      glue on a sheet of poster board to make a poster
      place under a sheet of butcher paper and do a crayon rubbing

Canvas Shoe Painting

  4+

Artists create separate and distinct paintings on left and right shoes with fabric paints to help distinguish and label left and right.

Materials
✓ white canvas tennis shoes
✓ fabric paints
✓ paintbrushes
✓ newspaper to cover floor

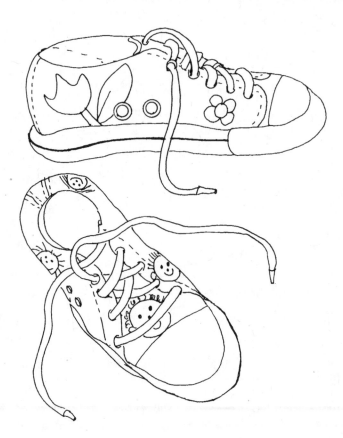

Process
1. Decide which shoe is the left and which is the right. Choose left first and set the right one aside.
2. Place the left white shoe on the newspaper so it can be painted.
3. Decorate the left shoe so that it will be markedly different from the right one, which will be decorated next. Think about differences in colors, shapes, opposites, letters, symbols, or numbers as decorations. Don't forget to decorate the shoelace too!
4. When the left shoe is decorated, bring out the right shoe. Keep the left one nearby for comparison.
5. Now decorate the right shoe completely different from the left.
6. Let both shoes dry completely.
7. Wear the shoes and focus on left and right while walking, turning, dancing, or marching.

Variations
- Decorate a plain T-shirt with fabric pens, using different approaches or designs on the front and the back.
- Decorate pants or shorts differently on each left or right leg.
- Decorate shoelaces for any pair of shoes to indicate left and right. Lace them back into the shoes when they have dried completely.
- Sew buttons or beads on mittens to indicate left and right.

**opposites
sculpture**

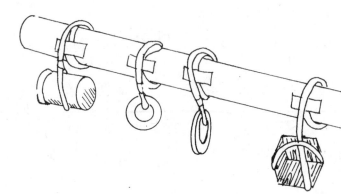

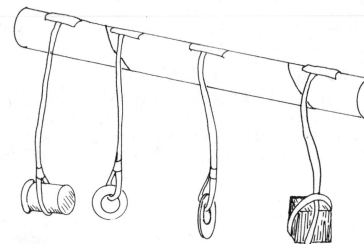

Up Down Around Mobile

A moving, active sculpture gives the young artist a firsthand experience exploring the directions of up, down, and around.

Materials
✓ sturdy cardboard tube
✓ 2' lengths of yarn (about 2, 3, or 4 per artist)
✓ collage items with some weight to tie on ends of the yarn strings, such as
    thread spools
    buttons
    nuts, washers, and other hardware
    pinecones
✓ tape

Process
1. Tape or tie a collage item to the end of a yarn string.
2. Make anywhere from two to four strings. Collage items may be the same on each string or different on each string.
3. Tape or tie each string to the cardboard tube. Tape them spaced apart but in line with each other.
4. Hold the tube in two hands, level, out in front of oneself.
5. Roll up the tube, keeping the tube level.
6. The yarn strings will roll up around the tube, and then can unroll back down.
7. Hang the tube as a mobile rolled up or rolled down.

Variations
■ Insert a wooden dowel through the tube and the tube can be rolled and unrolled easily.
■ Roll the yarn on a stick from outdoors.

Opposites Fold-Out Collage

Learning about opposites is also learning about how one thing relates to another.

Materials

✓ matte board, 2 pieces the same size
✓ wide tape
✓ white glue
✓ collage items, such as
     styrofoam packing materials, corks, beads, items gathered from outdoors,
     scraps of paper, stickers, pieces of clear self-adhesive paper,
     pieces of self-adhesive patterned paper, magazine pictures

Process

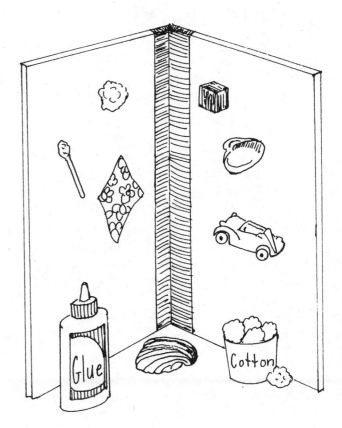

1. Tape two pieces of matte board together with wide tape on the backs. This will act like a hinge so the two pieces will stand when the two sides are brought in slightly (see illustration).
2. Place the matte board folder flat on the table.
3. Spread a variety of collage items out on a tray and place it on the table.
4. Examine the collage items. Think about words that are opposites to describe some of the collage items like big and little, long and short, soft and hard, fuzzy and rough.
5. After looking through the materials, start gluing opposite collage items on the folder, one on each side. For instance, a cotton ball would go on one side because it is soft, and a pebble would go on the other side because it is hard.
   Note: Some children will find opposites that adults have never considered, so be encouraging of all ranges of thinking.
6. Place the folder of opposites on a table or shelf so that it stands on its own.

Variation

■ Allow artists to think of obscure opposites. For example, a young learner may find a dog opposite a horse, an ocean opposite a lake, a bottle cap opposite a bead. Allow this kind of categorizing and encourage open thinking.

81

4+

**balance
sculpture**

Building Tower Sculpture

Boxes are taped together, giving the artist an experience with how one box relates to another for balance, height, and stability.

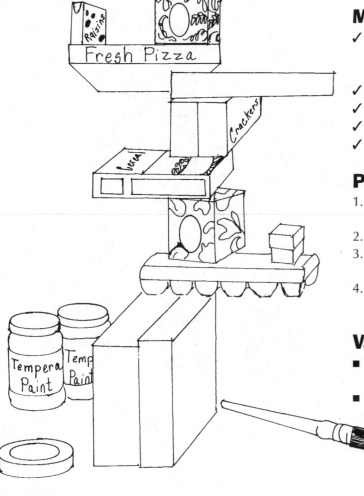

Materials
✓ empty cardboard containers and boxes, such as
> small cereal boxes, gift boxes, bath soap boxes, cornmeal boxes, milk cartons, shoe boxes, oatmeal boxes, jewelry boxes, egg cartons
✓ masking tape
✓ newspaper
✓ tempera paint in stable containers
✓ paintbrushes

Process
1. Paint the containers in any colorful way, with newspaper underneath to protect the floor or table.
2. The containers should dry completely.
3. When dry, stack the boxes and containers on, in, beside, and close to each other by building towers, castles, houses, or other sculptures or structures.
4. When satisfied with the sculpture, use masking tape to permanently join the boxes in a Building Tower Sculpture.

Variations
■ Paint small wooden blocks instead of cardboard boxes and glue the dry blocks together in a Tower Sculpture.
■ Glue any of the following items or other materials to create a tower sculpture:
> paper cups
> film containers
> paper tubes
> spools
> rolls of newsprint
> rocks

Spirobile

 **4+**

Children explore balance by gluing wood shavings and wood curls on threads and then suspending them from an embroidery hoop.

Materials
✓ wood shavings
✓ thread or string, cut in lengths of about 6" to 10"
✓ paper clip
✓ two pieces of thread about 12" long
✓ white glue
✓ embroidery hoop

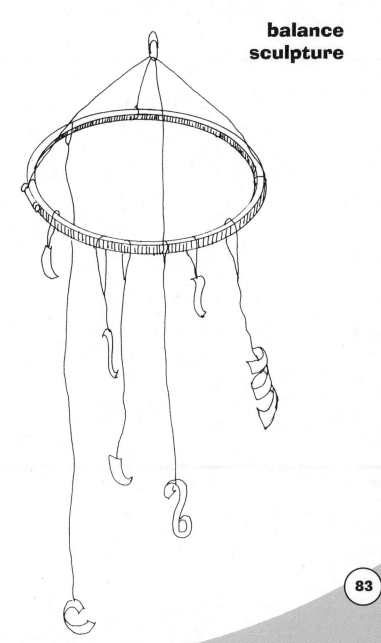

Process
1. Collect the curly wood shavings from a carpentry project. (Some excellent resources are high school wood shop class, cabinet shop, carpenter, lumber yard.) If not available, you may substitute small pieces of paper.
2. Cut one length of thread for each wood curl. Threads can all be exactly the same length or different lengths.
3. Place a drop of glue on any portion of one wood curl. Then put the end of a piece of thread in the glue. Do not disturb until dry. Do this for five or more wood curls.
4. When the glue has dried on the thread and the wood curl, take the other end of the thread and tie it to the inside ring of an embroidery hoop. Tie a slightly loose loop so the thread can be moved around the hoop if needed. Do the same with more wood curls.
5. For the hanging device of the mobile, tie one end of one piece of thread to the outer hoop. The other end should be tied directly across the hoop from the first end (see illustration).
6. To complete the hanging device, tie the second thread from one side of the hoop to the other, crossing the first thread.
7. Lay the outside hoop on the table and take the center of the threads where they cross, holding them together. Slip a paper clip over them both. Tie or loop the threads to the paper clip.
8. Put the two hoops back together and hang the mobile from the paper clip with the wood curls hanging down. Adjust the wood curls on the hoop so the hoop is balanced and the curls hang without touching.

83

4+

**balance
sculpture**

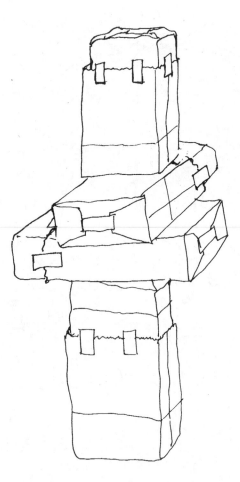

Grocery Bag Tower

Building a tower from homemade grocery bag blocks is an architectural challenge as artists discover how the blocks balance and relate to each other.

Materials
✓ brown paper grocery bags, lots of them
✓ newspaper
✓ sturdy tape (wide packing tape or wide masking tape)
✓ open area for building with the blocks

Process
1. Wad up newspaper and stuff a grocery bag.
2. Slide another bag over the open end of the first bag. An adult can tape around the seam with sturdy tape, such as packing tape or wide masking tape.
3. Create a large pile of the blocks.
4. Build, stack, and create any of the following:
   boat, tower, fort, hideout,
   tunnel, rocket, maze, fences,
   den, club house
5. When the group of architects have completely agreed it is time, the building project can be knocked down. As a further step, the blocks can be broken down and readied for recycling when they are no longer needed for building.

Variations
■ Use lunch bags instead of grocery bags for small blocks.
■ Combine other blocks in the building experience.

Exploring Spatial Relationships

Double Bubble Print

Bubbled shipping plastic is fun to pop, but first incorporate it into an interesting symmetrical print with paint.

Materials
✓ plastic bubble wrap
✓ stapler
✓ scissors
✓ trays filled with different colors of tempera paint
✓ paper, folded in half
✓ newspaper-covered drying and working areas

Process
1. Cut a piece of bubble plastic into two pieces the same size.
2. Staple them back to back with the bubbles on the outside.
3. Place a sheet of folded, then unfolded, paper on the work area.
4. Press one side of the bubble plastic into a tray of paint.
5. Turn over the bubble plastic and press the other side into the paint.
6. Lay the paint-filled bubble plastic on the paper, straight edge of the plastic against the fold line of the paper.
7. Fold the rest of the paper over the plastic and rub and press gently with both hands.
8. Unfold the paper, remove the bubbles, and look at the symmetrical print.

Variation
■ Come up with other materials that could produce symmetrical prints, such as:
   A piece of cardboard folded in half, cut in a design, and then unfolded.
   Yarn dipped in paint, placed on a sheet of paper near the fold, folded over, pressed, unfolded.
   Blobs of paint dropped on the fold of a paper, folded over, pressed, and then unfolded.

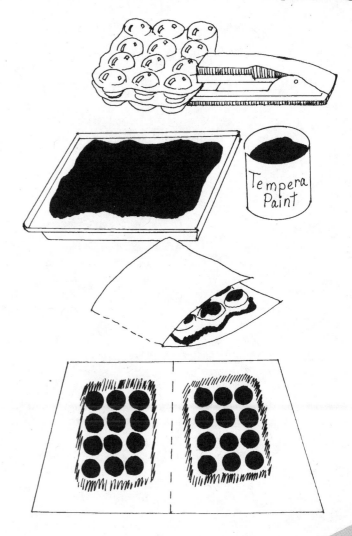

85

CHAPTER 5

Fences, Frames, Boxes

Math concepts explored in this chapter

Boundaries
Enclosure
Containment

In this chapter boundary means that objects are used to surround other objects, such as a star shape inside a circle shape or a picture framed with twigs. Enclosure is when objects are grouped together and fenced or held together as a unit, such as oranges in an orange crate, fish in an aquarium, or one child in a line of children. Young learners explore the concept of containment when an object is completely enclosed within another, such as a sandwich in a lunch box or people in a house.

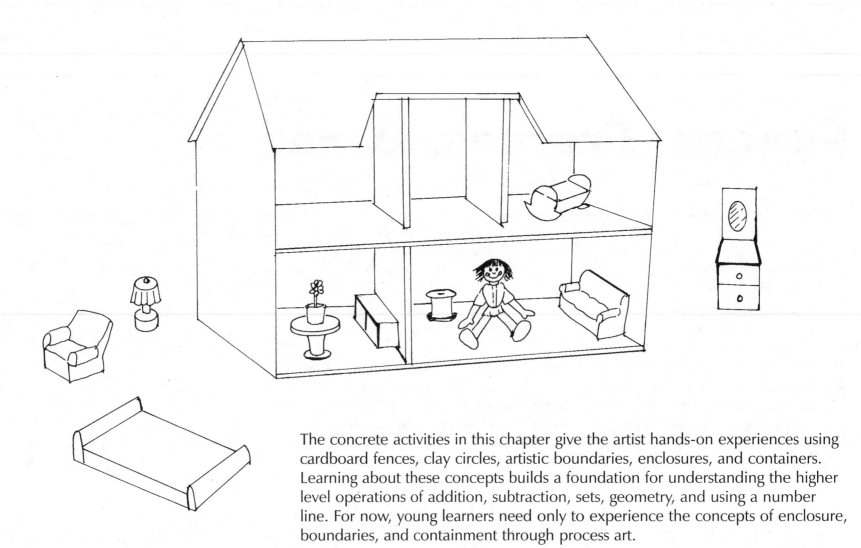

The concrete activities in this chapter give the artist hands-on experiences using cardboard fences, clay circles, artistic boundaries, enclosures, and containers. Learning about these concepts builds a foundation for understanding the higher level operations of addition, subtraction, sets, geometry, and using a number line. For now, young learners need only to experience the concepts of enclosure, boundaries, and containment through process art.

Encircle Me

boundaries
drawing

The traditional body tracing activity takes on new meaning as the concept of boundaries is explored through tracing, drawing, painting, and outlining.

Materials

✓ large sheets of craft paper, butcher paper, or newsprint
✓ crayons
✓ 2 people
✓ markers pens or paints and brushes
✓ construction paper or poster board (optional)

Process

1. The artist should lie down on a large sheet of craft paper, all parts and pieces of hands, feet, and hair completely enclosed on the paper with nothing sticking out or hanging over.
2. Another person traces around the body of the person on the paper.
3. When completely traced all the way around, the child paints the tracing.
4. Paint or color the details of the tracing. Be realistic or wildly colorful.
5. To save room, hang the painted body tracing on a wall or from a clothesline until dry.

Variation

■ Trace a group of smaller items on a piece of construction paper or poster board, such as
     soup cans
     kitchen tools
     lunch box
     hand or foot
Then paint or color the shapes. Cut them out and glue them inside the boundary of a circle shape drawn on a larger piece of paper.

4+

**boundaries
painting**

Sparkle Star

Star shapes glued within star shapes are enhanced with glitter as the concept of boundaries is explored with a shape within shape.

Materials
✓ tagboard or file folders
✓ scissors
✓ pencils
✓ big paper
✓ tempera paints and paint brushes
✓ glitter
✓ glue or brass fastener (optional)

Process
1. Draw a large star shape (or any large shape) on tagboard and cut it out. Adult help may be needed.
2. Put the large star (or any shape) aside.
3. Draw a small star shape (or other shape) on tagboard and cut it out.
4. Put the small star (or other shape) aside.
5. Place both star (or other) shapes on paper to use as a tracing pattern. Trace each pattern with a pencil.
6. Paint the stars (or shapes) which were traced on the paper in any colorful way. While the paint is still wet, sprinkle glitter over the shapes.
7. Stars or shapes should dry for several hours. When dry, cut out the painted stars or shapes.
8. Glue or fasten the small star or shape inside the large star or shape, using the glue or the brass fastener to hold them together.
9. If a brass fastener is used, the stars or shapes may be twirled and moved to add additional sparkle!

Variation
■ Draw freeform stars or other unique shapes.

Exploring Spatial Relationships

Inside Outside Collage

The young learner experiences the math concepts of boundaries and sorting through the art medium of collage.

Materials

✓ white glue
✓ large sheet of paper
✓ yarn
✓ collage items for gluing, such as
      packing materials
      bottle caps
      leaves
      buttons

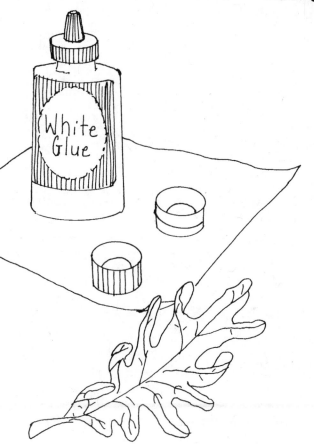

Process

1. Draw a big circle on the paper with the bottle of glue.
2. Place a piece of yarn in the glue, making an entire circle. If the yarn isn't long enough to make the entire circle, just add more pieces of yarn until it is a complete circle. Dry.
3. Sort collage items into piles, such as one pile of bottle caps, one pile of leaves, one of buttons.
4. Decide which piles will go inside the boundary of the yarn circle, and which will go outside the boundary of the yarn circle.
5. Glue items inside and outside the circle, creating a pattern or design.

Variations

■ Experiment with other items to group and then glue inside or outside the circle.
■ Experiment with substituting fabric, a hoop, or other materials for the yarn circle.
■ Create other borders or boundaries such as squares, cloud shapes, flower shapes with the yarn and glue.

4+ ◑

**boundaries
collage**

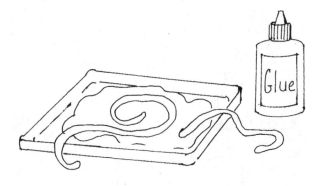

Boundary Collage

The artist draws or paints a design within the boundary of a yarn shape that has been glued on a piece of paper.

Materials
✓ cardboard square or styrofoam tray
✓ white glue
✓ nylon cord, cotton cord, or colorful yarn cut in different lengths (short lengths work best for young children)
✓ colorful colored paper
✓ markers or paints and brushes
✓ collage items (optional)
✓ newspaper-covered work area

Process
1. Pour a puddle of glue on the cardboard square or styrofoam tray.
2. Roll a short piece of string in the glue.
3. Place and arrange the sticky string on a sheet of colored paper, trying to make circles or shapes that are closed or making designs where the ends of the yarn strands cross over each other. Dry for about one hour.
4. When dry, add more interest and design to the yarn collage with colored markers or paint, coloring in the areas inside the yarn enclosures.
5. As an optional idea, add interest to the yarn enclosure by gluing collage items inside the shapes formed by the yarn. Dry.

Variations
■ Create string letters, names, or words.
■ Create string flowers or fish.
■ Create a stained glass window design.

Exploring Spatial Relationships

Tiny Twig Chalk Design

4+

Using the art medium of chalk combined with colorful twigs creates a collage that reinforces the concept of boundaries.

Materials
✓ tiny twigs
✓ tempera paints in several colors
✓ colored chalk or pastels
✓ colored construction paper (black or dark colors work well)
✓ white glue
✓ paintbrushes
✓ soft sponge pieces or facial tissue
✓ newspaper-covered work area

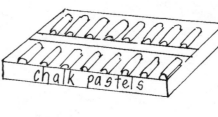

Process
1. Paint twigs with the tempera paints on the covered work area.
2. Leave in place and dry completely, usually several hours.
3. Next, draw a shape, design, or picture on the construction paper with the colored chalk.
4. Glue the colorful twigs around the chalk designs.
5. When the glue has dried, use a soft piece of sponge or a soft tissue to rub and blur the chalk lines. Add more chalk lines and blur those too, if desired.

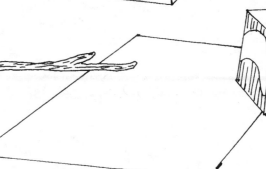

Variations
- Paint (or use as is) any of the following, instead of twigs
    tongue depressors, popsicle sticks, medical wooden spatulas, coffee stir sticks, thin wood scraps, wood shavings, toothpicks, craft sticks
- Make a design by gluing the painted twigs on matte board. Then encircle the twigs with any of the following ideas:
    Draw around the twigs with chalk or crayon.
    Paint lines around the twigs.
    Glue colorful yarn around the twigs.
    Outline the twigs with glue and any collage materials.

93

**boundaries
craft**

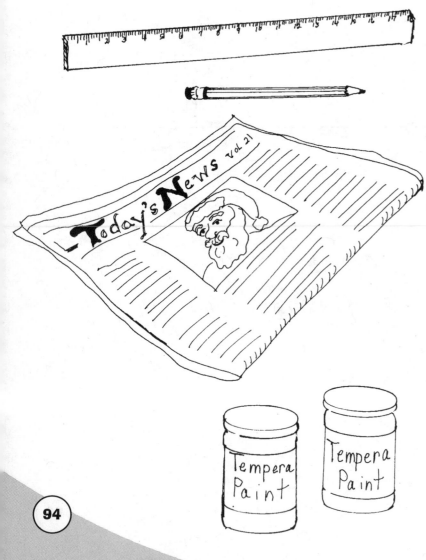

Papier-Mâché Frame

When young learners construct and create a papier-mâché picture frame, they are exploring the concept of boundaries.

Materials
- ✓ ruler
- ✓ pencil
- ✓ styrofoam tray
- ✓ scissors
- ✓ white glue solution (1/3 cup each glue and water) in a dish
- ✓ paintbrush
- ✓ newspaper
- ✓ paper clip
- ✓ tempera paint (at least 2 colors)
- ✓ pieces of sponge
- ✓ spray-on varnish (optional)
- ✓ heavy paper
- ✓ masking tape
- ✓ photograph or piece of artwork
- ✓ newspaper-covered work area
- ✓ wire rack

Process
1. Use the ruler and pencil to mark and measure a square shape in the middle of the styrofoam tray the size of the photo or artwork. Cut out the square with scissors (or an adult may use or assist with a craft knife).
2. Paint the entire front and back of the styrofoam tray with the glue solution.
3. Tear several sheets of newspaper into inch-wide strips, 4" to 6" long.
4. Paste these strips to the tray by first brushing glue on the tray, laying the newspaper strip on the glue, and then smoothing them with fingers.
5. Continue covering and overlapping newspaper strips on the tray, both front and back, until about three layers have been applied.
6. On the back of the frame, attach a paper clip for a hanger with a few pieces of glue-coated paper strips.

(Continued on next page)

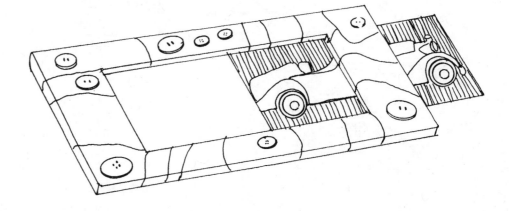

7. Dry the covered tray on a wire rack for several days. Turn it over now and then to help even out the drying and prevent sticking.

8. When dry, cover the frame with a coat or two of paint. Dry again.

9. Embellish the design by dabbing a sponge in a contrasting color of paint and then dabbing the tray. Dry again.

10. For a protective finish, an adult can spray a coating of varnish on the front and back of the frame. Do this outside or in a well-ventilated area.

11. Place a piece of heavy paper that is larger than the opening of the frame over the hole on the back of the frame. Tape it in place, leaving the top edge open.

12. Insert a photo or artwork in the pocket. Hang from the paper clip. (If the frame is very heavy be sure the paper clip is strong enough to support the frame.)

Variations

■ Glue decorative items to the frame such as yarn, glitter, sequins, confetti, or beads.
■ Decoupage magazine pictures or drawings on the frame instead of painting it.

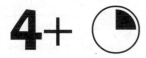

4+

**boundaries
craft**

Yarn Frame

When the young artist frames a personal drawing or painting, the concept of boundaries is explored.

Materials
✓ matte board
✓ pencils, pens, markers, crayons, paints and brushes
✓ yarn
✓ scissors
✓ white glue
✓ optional materials, such as
  glitter, colored glue, colored sand,
  sequins, confetti, holes punched from paper

Process
1. Draw or paint a picture on the matte board.
2. Cut yarn into manageable lengths.
3. To create a frame around the picture, glue yarn around the outer edge of the matte board in any design or pattern.
4. Add glitter, colored glue, colored sand, sequins, or confetti to the yarn frame to enhance the design.
5. Dry overnight.

Variations
■ Glue a photograph on a piece of matte board, leaving a border of blank matte board around the photo. Frame the photo with fancy drawings, colored tape, colored glue, buttons, sewing trims, or other materials.
■ Ask a frame shop to save matte frames for art use. Decorate these to place around paintings or special photos. The paintings or photos can be changed at any time and a new one highlighted in the frame.
■ Frame the artwork with wood scraps from a framing shop.

Exploring Spatial Relationships

Circle Square, Square Circle

The young learner uses play dough to produce circles and squares that fit inside each other, reinforcing the idea of enclosure.

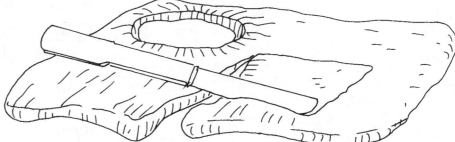

Materials
✓ modeling clay or play dough in assorted colors
✓ covered work area
✓ rolling pin (optional)
✓ plastic knife
✓ matte board
✓ scissors (optional)
✓ glue (optional)

Process
1. Flatten the clay or play dough by hand or with a rolling pin on the covered work area.
2. Cut the clay or play dough into a variety of different sizes of squares and circles with the plastic knife. Place a circle on the matte board, and then a slightly smaller square on the circle.
3. Then, in a separate pile, stack a smaller circle on the square and so on. Stacks of two, or more than two, are effective.
4. Make further designs combining circles and squares. Press the playdough or clay firmly and it will stick to the matte board.

Variations
- Use construction paper to create circles and squares and glue them onto contrasting construction paper.
- Use other materials to cut and assemble as shapes upon shapes, such as
    fabric scraps
    felt
    wrapping paper
    thin vinyl or foam board
    foil
    different sizes of labels

97

enclosure craft

Knots, Knots, Knots

The knotted rope resembles points on a number line. The artist selects which knots will receive a feather and which will not, creating a knot design. The feathers are also enclosed between the knots.

Materials
✓ yarn, rope, string, or twine
✓ scissors
✓ craft feathers

Process
1. Cut yarn or string to a manageable length.
2. Tie a row of knots on the yarn in any fashion, although not too tight. Leave enough give in the knot to insert a feather.
3. Slide a feather through each knot at different intervals.
4. Pull the knots tighter around the feather.
5. Make one string of feathers, or make many strings of feathers. Give each knot a feather, or skip knots so some have no feathers. This is an open-ended activity.
6. Tie the ends of the feathered string into a necklace, or join many feathered strings together into a garland to decorate a wall, window, door, climbing toy, or tree. (While creating, talk about which knots have feathers and which ones do not. Find knots that are between feathers and feathers that are between knots.)

Variations
■ Cut long strips of fabric from scraps. Tie them in knots, but within each knot, tie a ribbon, bead, button, or other pretty sewing trim.
■ Play "I'm a Necklace" with a group of children. Extend a giant loop "necklace" of rope and place it on the floor. Children space themselves around the rope and pick it up. Each child is a "bead." Call children's names to come inside the circle, or to be like beads on the necklace.
■ Place a feather or bead in every knot, every two knots, every fifth knot, and so on.

Exploring Spatial Relationships

Box Assemblage

An assemblage is similar to a collage but uses three-dimensional materials, such as cans, cups, wood scraps, and boxes. Creating an assemblage inside a box reinforces the concept of enclosure.

enclosure assemblage

Materials

✓ a cardboard box or an orange crate
✓ pieces of wood scraps
✓ odds and ends, such as
    soda cans, straws, small boxes, paper cups,
    beads, jar lids, framing scraps, paper plates, spools
✓ lots of glue, nails and hammer, tape (hot glue gun with adult assistance)
✓ paints
✓ paintbrushes
✓ newspaper-covered work area

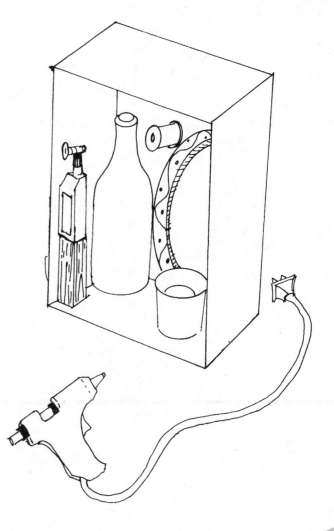

Process

1. Choose the pieces of wood and odds and ends for the assemblage.
2. Place them in the box.
3. Move them about until the arrangement takes shape. Then start gluing and taping them in place. (An adult can assist with a hot glue gun if desired.) Let the glue dry for an hour or so.
4. Paint the assemblage in the box a variety of colors, or paint it all the same color. Each technique looks completely different in its effect. Dry overnight.
5. The box assemblage can be displayed standing on one end like a window or door, or displayed flat on a table or counter. Give the assemblage a name, if desired.

Variations

■ Visit a lumber yard or high school wood shop class for a unique selection of wood scraps.
■ Frame shops often have beautiful and unusual framing scraps and matte scraps to give away.

4+

**enclosure
craft**

 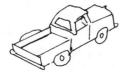

Basket Displays

Decorating and designing individual baskets with paints is a colorful, creative technique to explore enclosure.

Materials
- ✓ baskets, any variety of natural baskets
- ✓ nontoxic acrylic paints and paintbrushes
- ✓ newspaper-covered work area
- ✓ jar or block to use as a drying rack
- ✓ items for filling the baskets, such as
        fruit or nuts, small toys, silk flowers,
        costume jewelry, marbles, real flowers
- ✓ ribbon, raffia, strips of fabric (optional)

Process
1. Paint baskets as desired with the acrylic paints and brushes.
2. Leave in place on the covered work area and dry several hours or overnight. Place the basket upside-down over a jar or block so the bottom of the basket won't stick to the table.
3. When dry, fill each basket with gifts or other items, enclosing them within the basket.
4. Further decorate the basket with ribbon, raffia, or strips of fabric (optional).

Variation
- Use a theme for filling a basket, such as
        Black and White
        Soft
        Colors I Love
        Favorites
        My Best Toy Cars
        Collections
        Beads I Made
        Holidays
        Shiny and Dull
        Buttons

Flower Power

The young artist experiments with different arrangements of flowers and manipulates the possibilities of design within the enclosure.

Materials
✓ any kind of flowers, such as
   silk
   straw
   paper
   plastic
✓ magazines with photos of flowers (optional)
✓ ball of clay
✓ vase, basket, or other container
✓ heavy scissors to cut flower stems (adult help may be needed)
✓ sewing trims (optional)

Process
1. Assemble a box of silk, plastic, or straw flowers; use ones with flexible stems. Those that do not bend may still work.
2. Look through magazines and books to see flower arrangements. Cut out a few pictures to look at for ideas, if desired.
3. Place a ball of clay in the vase or container of choice. Start arranging flowers by sticking the stems into the clay to hold flowers upright and in any desired shape or design. Cut or bend stems, creating a floral design.
4. When satisfied with the flower arrangement, add a ribbon or other sewing trims to further decorate the container or leave the container plain.

Variations
■ Arrange fresh flowers.
■ Arrange dry flowers, grasses, weeds, and reeds.
■ Make paper flowers with pipe cleaner stems and arrange.
■ Make unconventional flowers out of throwaways such as used film canisters, curlers, bottle caps, or checkers.

enclosure construction

Cardboard Fences

The artist creates a fanciful arrangement of plastic or toy figures in the enclosure of a cardboard box.

Materials
✓ shallow cardboard boxes or lids from shoe boxes
✓ plastic animals, people, or cars, or small toy figures
✓ tempera paints and paintbrushes
✓ craft glue (or hot glue gun with adult supervision)
✓ paper scraps

Process
1. Paint the inside of a cardboard box or a lid from a shoe box in a colorful way. Some artists enjoy painting the box lid to resemble green grass or some other outdoor area with the sides of the box like a fenced area.
2. Dry completely, usually several hours.
3. Create an arrangement in the boundaries of the painted box with the toys.
4. When satisfied with the arrangement, glue the figures or toys to the box with craft glue. Dry. (An adult can use a hot glue gun instead of using craft glue.)
5. Add other little items to the scene such as trees made of paper scraps or a pond made from aluminum foil.
6. Display, use as a table centerpiece, or join with other fenced projects to create a table filled with sprawling fenced properties in one huge landscape.

Variations
■ Place a plastic fruit basket over animal figurines to create a zoo.
■ Make roads, stop signs, bridges, and parking lots for very little toy cars.
■ Collect tiny plastic items from cake decorations or party favors to use in the fence design.

Exploring Spatial Relationships

See-Through Scrimshaw Boxes

Nesting containers are created from plastic jugs and canisters, using an adaptation of scrimshaw (originally a decorative technique of scratching a design with a sharp tool into bone that was then rubbed with colored inks).

Materials
✓ plastic (transparent or semitransparent) containers, such as
     milk jugs, cooking oil containers,
     empty prescription pill bottles, liter bottles
✓ X-acto knife (adult use only)
✓ scratching tools, (with assistance) such as
     nails, short screwdriver, paper clips
✓ ink pads in a variety of colors
✓ sponge pieces or makeup sponges
✓ paper towels

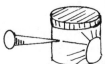

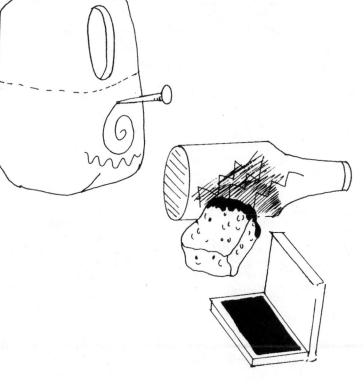

Process
1. The adult should carefully cut away the tops of the plastic containers with the X-acto knife.
2. Remove labels from containers by washing or soaking. Then dry.
3. Scratch designs into the plastic containers with any or all of the scratching tools. Be careful when pushing on the tool that it doesn't slip and poke. Brush away any scrapings.
4. Using a sponge, dab color from the ink pad.
5. Dab and rub the color from the sponge into the scratches in the plastic.
6. Before the ink can dry for too long, take a paper towel and rub away as much ink from the container as possible. Most of the ink will remain in the scratches rather than on the smooth surface.
7. When the containers are decorated, experiment with nesting the containers, one inside another, smallest container inside the next larger container and so on.
8. Containers can also be used for storage of a variety of sizes of items and lined up in order of their sizes.

Variation
■ Plastic containers can be decorated with permanent markers.

(103)

4+ ◗

containment drawing

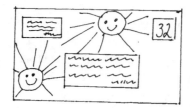

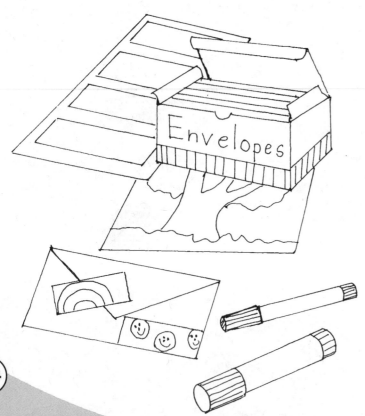

Fancy Mail

Creating real mail to be delivered to a person is an intriguing way to explore the concept of containment with the envelope being the container.

Materials
✓ sheet of blank address labels, stick-on variety
✓ plain white envelope
✓ any paper
✓ drawing materials, especially markers

Process
1. Design and color the blank stick-on address labels while still on the label sheet.
2. Create colorful shapes, designs, names, numbers, letters, or scribbles on each label. Keep at least two labels blank, one for the address and one to hold a blank space for the postage stamp and postal cancel.
3. When lots of labels are ready, stick them to the envelope in any pattern or design, decorating the envelope. Place one blank label on the envelope approximately where a real address would go on an envelope. Place the other blank label in the upper right corner to hold a place for the postage stamp and postal cancel. Set the envelope aside.
4. Dictate a letter, draw a picture, or create a design on the paper.
5. Fold the paper and place it in the envelope.
6. Address or label the letter with someone's name. Give it to them in person or mail it. Don't forget a stamp if it is mailed!

Variation
■ Create cards for special occasions, such as
 Birthday
 Valentine's Day
 First Day of Spring
 Lost Tooth Day
 Mother's Day
 Sad Day
 I Love You
 Good-Bye

Can Inside Can Inside Can...

The artist experiences and explores the concept of containment by freely dabbing paints from sponges and fingers onto assorted sizes of soup cans, coffee cans, or vegetable and fruit cans.

Materials

✓ nontoxic acrylic paints (because they stick to metal)
✓ cans in assorted sizes, clean and free of rough edges (Try to find about 5 cans that fit one into another, such as tomato paste can in tomato sauce can in soup can in larger soup can in coffee can. Cans should be washed and dried, with labels removed.)
✓ sponges cut into pieces (to fit in small hands)
✓ newspaper
✓ water

Process

1. Squeeze acrylic paints in blobs on the newspaper.
2. Dip dampened sponges into the paints, mixing colors if desired.
3. Dab sponges on the cans to give them color and design.
4. Dry. Meanwhile, wash hands and sponges.
5. When the cans are dry, nest smaller cans into larger cans.
6. Nest and unnest, stack and unstack.
7. Use cans to hold things such as pencils, art supplies, sewing trims, or pieces of toys. Line them up in order according to size on a desk or windowsill, stack them like a sculpture, or nest them for a playful activity.

Variations

■ Use brushes instead of sponges to paint the cans.
■ Cover the cans with paper and then dab tempera paints on the covered cans.
■ Cover cans with drawings and then with clear self-adhesive paper to seal in the drawings.

105

4+

containment craft

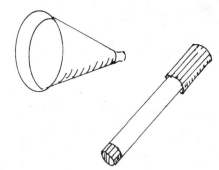

Cascarones (Confetti Eggs)

Empty egg shells are filled with confetti to capture the concept of containment in this traditional Easter and Fiesta celebration from San Antonio, Texas.

Materials
✓ eggs and egg carton
✓ bowl
✓ water and towels
✓ Easter egg dye or colored markers, white crayon
✓ materials to fill and decorate eggs
      crepe paper, tissue paper, shredded paper,
      paper hole punches, scrap paper, Easter grass,
      confetti, foil paper
✓ scissors
✓ white glue
✓ plastic funnel with hole about the size of a nickel

Process
1. With adult help, tap the top of an egg gently on a hard surface. (Be ready to catch an egg that breaks too much!) Make a small hole about the size of a nickel and no larger than a quarter in the shell.
2. Pour out the insides of the egg shell in a bowl and refrigerate the contents to cook and eat later. Do this for as many eggs as will be used.
3. Carefully rinse out the egg shells with water. Let them dry on a towel or in the egg carton.
4. Gently color the shells with Easter egg dye or markers. Make patterns, designs, words, or pictures. Gently (very gently!) drawing with the crayon on the shell and then dying it will create a resist design. Then dry again.
5. While the shells are drying, prepare the filling for the shells. Use a hole punch or patterned craft punches to make lots and lots of confetti. (Or use commercial confetti.)
6. Cut any of the following into tiny bits: scrap paper, tissue or crepe paper, Easter grass, foil, or other papers. Mix them all together or keep them separate as you like.

(Continued on next page)

Exploring Spatial Relationships

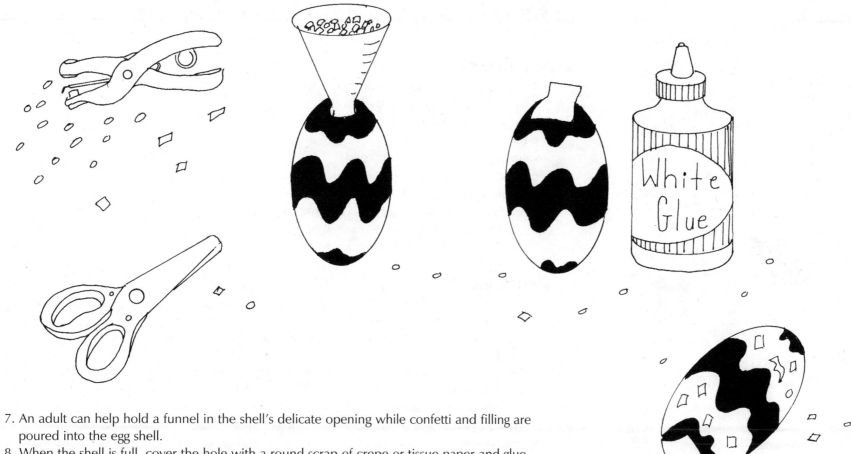

7. An adult can help hold a funnel in the shell's delicate opening while confetti and filling are poured into the egg shell.

8. When the shell is full, cover the hole with a round scrap of crepe or tissue paper and glue. Dry in the egg carton. (Add additional decoration to the outside of the shell by gluing on bits of paper if desired.)

9. The most fun of all, with permission, is to gently throw the eggs like they do in San Antonio, Texas, at Easter and Fiesta. The confetti explodes from its boundaries and brings celebration and laughter to all who agree to participate.

Fences, Frames, Boxes

4+ ◑

**containment
construction**

Shake 'Em Boxes

Combining listening experiences with mathart broadens the depth of creativity in this construction and painting activity.

Materials
✓ small lightweight containers with lids, such as
   cornmeal containers, shoe boxes,
   oatmeal containers, jewelry boxes
✓ paper and tape
✓ rubber stamps, colorful stamp pads
✓ colored masking tape or craft tape
✓ permanent markers
✓ items to enclose inside the containers, such as
   jingle bells, coins, small plastic blocks,
   plastic bottle caps, nuts and bolts

Process
1. Press the rubber stamps onto the ink pads and then on the paper, creating designs and patterns to decorate the chosen containers.
2. Cover the lightweight containers with the decorated paper and tape. Cover the lids too, if desired.
3. Place some of the items inside the container and then add the lid. Secure the lid with colored masking tape to seal the contents inside the container.
4. Shake the container and create rhythmic sounds.
5. Have a parade or accompany a favorite piece of music!

Variation
■ Cut open a dried gourd with adult help. Fill it with pebbles, rice, or other noisy items. Tape it closed. Paint it and use it for a musical shaker.

CHAPTER 6

Parts and Pieces

Math concepts explored in this chapter

The Whole and Its Parts
Separation
Division

The young child experiences the concept of separation when a cookie is broken in two pieces to share with a friend, when grapes are pulled from the bunch into individual and separate grapes, or when a puzzle is taken apart and put together again. All these experiences lead to a sense of the whole as a single distinct object that is then separated into its parts, or when the parts are put together to form a whole. In addition, the number "one" must be understood as having the characteristics of 1 item, 1 button, 1 loaf of bread, 1 pizza, and so on before it can be segmented into 2 or more parts.

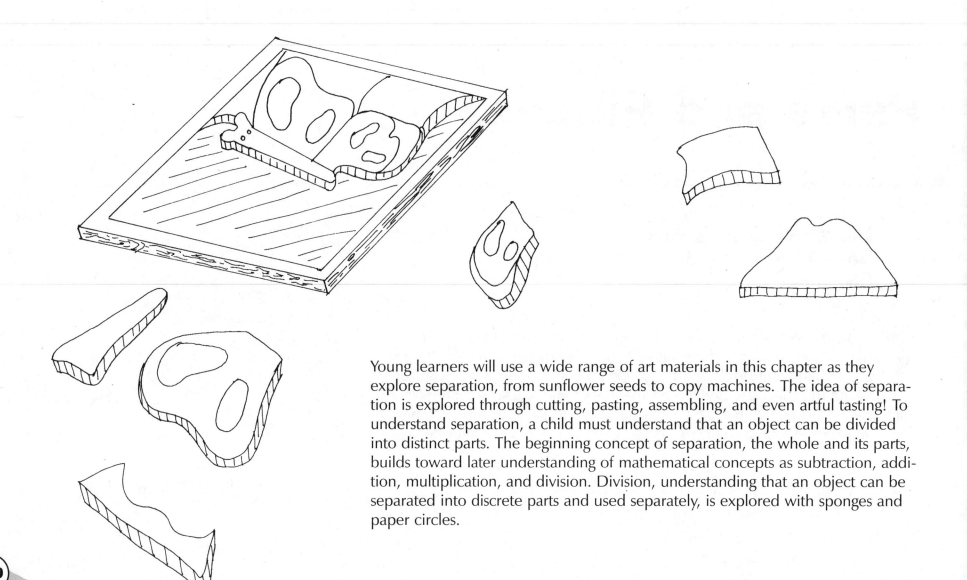

Young learners will use a wide range of art materials in this chapter as they explore separation, from sunflower seeds to copy machines. The idea of separation is explored through cutting, pasting, assembling, and even artful tasting! To understand separation, a child must understand that an object can be divided into distinct parts. The beginning concept of separation, the whole and its parts, builds toward later understanding of mathematical concepts as subtraction, addition, multiplication, and division. Division, understanding that an object can be separated into discrete parts and used separately, is explored with sponges and paper circles.

Puzzle Put Together

By creating an individual puzzle from an original drawing and using it over and over to see how parts of a whole fit together, a young learner will begin to understand the concept of the whole and its parts.

the whole and its parts
drawing

Materials

✓ heavy paper or file folder
✓ crayons, markers, pencils, pens
✓ scissors
✓ plastic sandwich bag, large envelope, or hosiery box

Process

1. Create a drawing with crayons, markers, pencils, or pens on the heavy paper.
2. When complete, cut the drawing into five or six simple, broad puzzle pieces with the scissors.
3. Put the puzzle drawing back together again on the table.
4. Store the puzzle in a sandwich bag, large envelope, or hosiery box to be used again.

Variations

■ Glue a magazine picture to a heavy piece of paper. When dry, cut the picture apart, creating a puzzle that can be used again and again.

■ Create a Strips Puzzle by gluing a magazine picture to a 6″ x 9″ piece of heavy paper. Cut the picture into 1″ to 2″ wide strips. Put the puzzle back together inside a 6″ x 9″ hosiery box. For an extra sturdy puzzle, first cover the glued picture with clear self-adhesive paper and then cut it apart or into strips.

■ Create a puzzle from a photograph, poster, or completed dry painting.

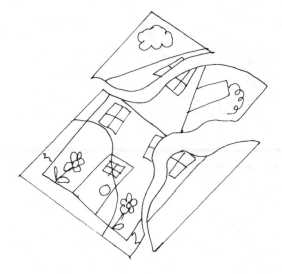

4+ ◑ ✋

**the whole and its parts
painting**

Partner Square Painting

Chalk grid lines are snapped on the paper forming sections that are then painted. The design comes together and shows how the sectioned parts of the paper make up the whole design.

Materials
✓ newsprint to protect floor
✓ butcher paper taped to floor, about 3' x 3' square
✓ sidewalk chalk
✓ 4' length of heavy twine
✓ tempera paints and paintbrushes
✓ aprons or shirts to cover artists
✓ 2 or 3 children

Process
1. Cover about a 5' x 5' area of floor with newsprint to protect from spills.
2. Tape a large square of butcher paper to the center of the newsprint.
3. Stretch a length of twine between two artists. A third artist rubs chalk back and forth on the twine until it is well coated with chalk.
4. The two artists kneel on either side of the large square of paper, holding the twine tight across the paper at floor level.
5. For the amazing fun moment, one of the partners or a third person lifts the center of the twine a few inches and then lets it snap back to the paper, leaving a chalk line on the paper.
6. Repeat the chalking of the twine. This time, move the twine over about 5" to 6" and snap again.
7. Repeat about six times, then cross over the first lines so that the squares appear on the paper each time (see illustration). It is common for the shapes to resemble squares but not quite be true squares. Working together is difficult!
8. When the paper is covered with chalked squares, paint the squares with tempera paints. Leave some squares blank, if desired. Leave in place and dry several hours.
9. When dry, notice how the parts of the squares make up a whole; the large butcher paper square is sectioned with many colorful smaller squares.

Variation
■ Segment a chalkboard or sidewalk into a grid and use colored chalk to color in the squares.

112

Break Away Clay

4

This clay relief experience helps the child understand the concept of the whole and its parts as pieces of clay come together to form a whole design.

Materials

✓ modeling clay in bright colors
✓ plastic knives and other modeling tools (optional)
✓ newspaper-covered work area
✓ scrap matte board squares, any sizes

Process

1. Start with single larger hunks of clay in several colors.
2. Break off smaller pieces of clay from each whole, larger piece.
3. Use these pieces to press onto the matte board to create a design, picture, or clay relief. The clay will stick without any help.
4. Break off more pieces and press these to the board and to the clay already on the board.
5. When satisfied with the exploration and creating, the design may be displayed upright. The clay will not fall off if it was pressed firmly to the board.

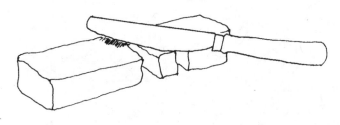

Variations

- Start with several small individual pieces of clay and form a large single shape.
- Create a Breakaway Clay design on a piece of Plexiglas or see-through easel board.
- Create a clay relief as before, but this time, do so on the back of the glass in a picture frame. When the glass is turned over, the pressed and flat colorful design will look amazingly different on the "wrong" side. (Be careful that the glass stays flat on the covered table while creating so it doesn't break. Or use plastic instead of glass.)

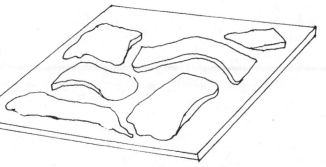

4+ ◔

**the whole and its parts
sculpture**

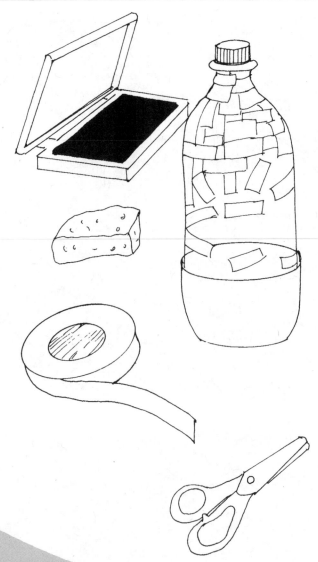

Tape Pieces Sculpture

Masking tape readily transforms a plastic jug or bottle into a useful, leather-looking vase or container.

Materials
✓ masking tape
✓ scissors
✓ plastic jug or liter bottle
✓ colorful ink pad and sponge (shoe polish may be used)
✓ cloth

Process
1. Pull off a long piece of masking tape from the roll.
2. Stick one end of the long piece to the table.
3. From the other end, snip or tear off smaller pieces from the larger piece.
4. Stick each small piece to the plastic jug, overlapping edges. Cover the entire jug from the pouring spout all the way down and across the bottom.
5. Rub a sponge on a colorful ink pad and then rub and dab the ink-filled sponge on the masking tape pieces covering the jug. Mix colors from different ink pads, if desired.
6. When satisfied with the inking of the jug, rub the entire jug with a cloth to remove any excess ink and polish a bit.
7. Use the jug as a vase or other decorative container.

Variations
■ Use masking tape pieces on wood, plastic, rocks, or other surfaces.
■ Use other types of tape such as library tape, craft tape, and duct tape.
■ Create the sculpture with colored masking tape such as pink, blue, green, and yellow.

Parts and Pieces Relief

 4+

Sculpting with sorted wood pieces appeals to artists who like to create a large, three-dimensional piece.

Materials

✓ scraps of wood, any sizes
✓ flat scrap of wood for base of relief
✓ framing scraps, some small and some long enough to frame the flat scrap
✓ white glue (hot glue gun works well with adult help)
✓ hand saw
✓ white latex enamel paint (washable) and wide brush
✓ gold or silver touch-up color (washable) and small brush
✓ newspaper-covered work area in a well-ventilated area
✓ washing tub, towels, sink
✓ screw in eye-hook, heavy piece of wire or strong cord for hanging relief

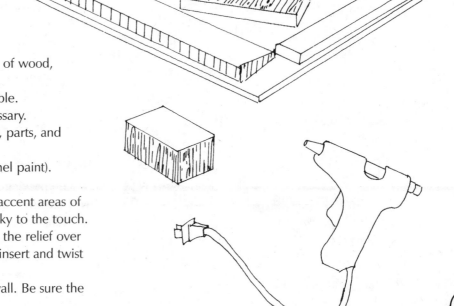

Process

1. Place the flat piece of wood on the covered work area. Sort through the scraps of wood, setting aside pieces to use for the relief.
2. First outline the flat piece of wood with framing scraps that are as long as possible.
3. Have an adult use a hand saw to shorten pieces to fit around the edge, if necessary.
4. Next, glue wood scraps inside the frame, filling all the empty space with scraps, parts, and pieces. When the entire board is covered, let it dry overnight or several hours.
5. When dry, paint the entire relief with white latex enamel paint (washable enamel paint).
6. Dry overnight. Meanwhile, cleanup and wash and dry the paintbrush.
7. When the relief is dry or nearly dry, use the smaller paintbrush to touch-up or accent areas of the relief with gold or silver washable paint. Dry completely until no longer sticky to the touch.
8. Clean brushes and all work areas. When the gold or silver paint has dried, turn the relief over and screw in two eye-hooks on either side of the flat piece at the edges. Then insert and twist wire through the eye-hooks to create a strong hanger.
9. Hang the Parts and Pieces Relief outdoors on a wall or fence or indoors on a wall. Be sure the hanger is strong enough to support the relief.

115

4+ ◔

the whole and its parts collage

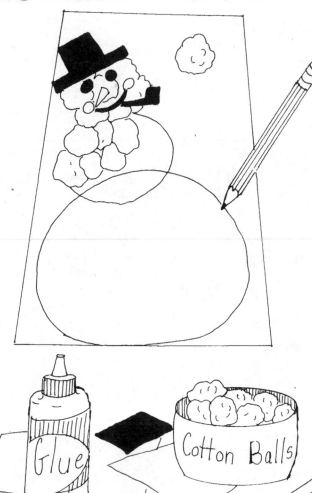

Cotton Ball Design

Cotton balls make up a whole cotton ball design and help reinforce the concept of the whole and its parts.

Materials
✓ paper
✓ pencil
✓ white glue
✓ cotton balls (white or colored)
✓ scissors
✓ paper scraps

Process
1. Draw a shape on the paper. (Sometimes it is fun to create a cotton ball snowman, snow-woman, or cotton ball cloud shape.) Fill in the shape with white glue.
2. Place cotton balls in the glue, filling the shape until it is covered with cotton.
3. Place other details on the cotton design by cutting paper scraps into shapes and pieces. Do not glue yet.
4. Notice that the parts and pieces make a whole. Move the parts and pieces around to change the design. (Snowmen and women might like eyes, nose, hat, scarf.)
5. When satisfied with the design, add more glue and stick the parts and pieces to the cotton ball design.

Variations
- Use packing material instead of cotton balls. Paint with tempera paints, if desired.
- Glue any collage items into a shape. Add further collage items as decoration.
- Think of other "whole and its parts" that might be fun to create, such as
     a tree design, with fruit or blossoms
     a fish bowl design, with fish
     a clown design, with legs, arms, big shoes, attached with brads

Above and Below Ribbon Mural

A long strip of butcher paper is divided into two sections by a wide length of bright ribbon. The artist then glues collage materials above and below the ribbon to reinforce the concept of the whole mural and its parts.

Materials

✓ wall for a work surface
✓ long strip of butcher paper (sold on a roll at the grocery store)
✓ tape
✓ wide ribbon, the same length as the strip of butcher paper
✓ white glue
✓ collage materials (especially self-stick materials), such as
   stickers, labels, paper reinforcements, self-adhesive paper pieces,
   pieces of colored masking tape,
   lick-&-stick stamps from book clubs, record clubs, wildlife groups,
   pieces of colored library tape,
   paper scraps, magazine pictures

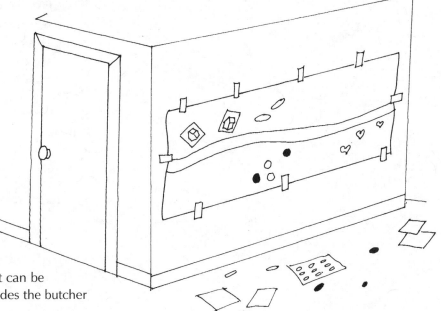

Process

1. Tape the long strip of butcher paper to the wall at child height.
2. Glue a long, wide ribbon in the center of entire length of the butcher paper. It can be attached as one straight line or looped and curled along the way, just so it divides the butcher paper in half, top and bottom.
3. Artists glue, tape, or stick selections of collage materials above and below the ribbon, creating patterns or designs.

Variations

■ From a stiff piece of cardboard, hang collage items attached to yarn that will hang below the cardboard, and attach stiff objects that will stand up above the cardboard.
■ Explore other opposites in a collage, such as in and out, up and down, high and low, backward and forward, over and under, left and right, inside and outside, this way and that way.

117

3+ ◑ ✋

the whole and its parts collage

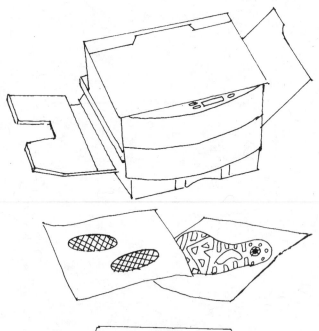

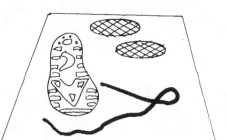

Copier Collage

Many parts and pieces of paper designs created on a photocopy machine are cut and assembled into one paper collage, giving the young artist experience in how the parts make up the whole.

Materials
✓ photocopy machine
✓ unused side of used paper
✓ items to copy (look for objects with textures and shapes), such as
    baskets (natural or plastic), cheese cloth, rubber bands, sandpaper,
    sewing trims, corks, sponges, marbles, yarn, shoe treads, paper shapes, odds and ends
✓ scissors
✓ paste
✓ matte board for the base
✓ crayons, colored pencils, or colored markers

Process
1. Place the chosen objects on the copier tray of the photocopy machine. Make one or two copies of each item.
2. Spread the copies out on a work space.
3. Cut the copies into the shapes of the real objects and paste them on the matte board to create a design, portrait, landscape, or crazy collage.
4. When the paste has dried, use crayons, markers, or colored pencils to add color to the Copier Collage.

Variations
■ Create a Copier Theme Collage, such as
    Sewing Collage from scraps of fabric and sewing items
    Kitchen Collage from kitchen utensils, foods, packages, cans
    Toy Collage from toy parts, packages, boxes, and puzzles
    Litter Collage from things collected outside
■ Assemble a selection of items on the copier surface and copy the assemblage. Color or paint the resulting design.

Patches Appliqué

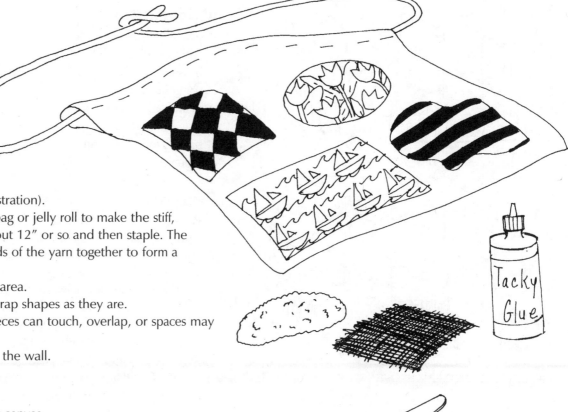

the whole and its parts craft

4+

U se pieces and patches of fabric scraps to design a wall hanging which reinforces the idea that many parts make up a whole.

Materials

✓ long strip of burlap, felt, or plain fabric (about 1' x 3')
✓ piece of yarn (about 1 yd. long)
✓ stapler
✓ fabric scraps
✓ scissors
✓ fabric glue or tacky glue
✓ newspaper-covered work area

Process

1. Stretch the large piece of fabric out on the floor.
2. Place the yarn across the top edge of the fabric (see illustration).
3. Begin rolling the fabric around the yarn like a sleeping bag or jelly roll to make the stiff, heavier top edge of the wall hanging. Roll the fabric about 12" or so and then staple. The yarn will be hanging out the ends of the roll. Tie the ends of the yarn together to form a hanger above the roll. Adult help may be needed.
4. Move the wall hanging to the newspaper-covered work area.
5. Cut scraps of fabric or felt into new shapes or use the scrap shapes as they are.
6. Glue the shapes to the wall hanging with fabric glue. Pieces can touch, overlap, or spaces may be left between them.
7. When dry, hang the wall hanging from the yarn loop on the wall.

Variations

■ Sew scraps on a base fabric such as a piece of muslin or canvas.
■ Attach and outline fabric scraps with fabric glue that comes in colors from craft and hobby stores.

119

the whole and its parts craft

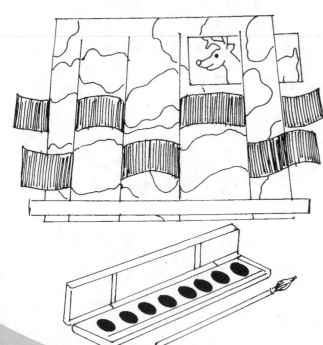

Watercolor Plus Weaving

In the watercolor plus weaving technique young learners explore weaving patterns, how the colors of weaving strips affect color and design, and how the parts make up its whole complete form.

Materials
✓ watercolor paints
✓ white paper
✓ brushes
✓ water in cups
✓ plain construction paper
✓ magazine pictures
✓ scissors (or paper cutter for adult use)
✓ tape

Process
1. Paint a watercolor painting on the white paper with a paintbrush. Dry completely. If very wrinkled, with adult help, iron to flatten with a dry iron on medium.
2. For the weaving strips, cut paintings, magazine pictures, and construction paper into 1" to 2" wide strips.
3. From the watercolor painting, cut ½" to 1" wide slits starting at one edge and stopping just before the other edge. The slits may be straight, wiggly, or zigzaggy. One edge will be cut open and loose, the other end will still be together and uncut. (See illustration.)
4. Tape the uncut edge of the watercolor painting to the table to control the weaving.
5. Weave the loose strips under and over the painting strips taped to the table. Use any pattern or weaving idea. "Over, under" is a common weaving pattern, but any pattern is acceptable.
6. Slide each loose strip up toward the uncut end of the weaving. Secure with tape at each side edge.

Variations
- Cover the weaving with clear self-adhesive paper for a mat that can be sponged clean.
- Add sprinkles of salt to the watercolor painting before it dries.
- Weave painting strips through an old poster as the weaving sheet.

Sunflower Seed Separation

Young learners remove sunflower seeds from the head of a ripe, mature sunflower and separate them into hundreds of seeds to help them understand the concept of separation.

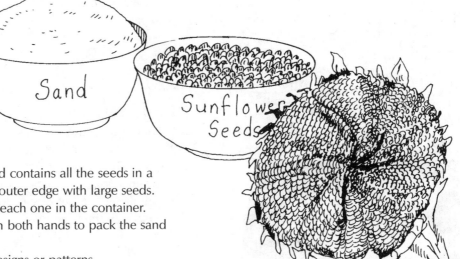

Materials

✓ ripe, full head of a sunflower plant, dried
✓ container to hold sunflower seeds
✓ sand in a flat metal baking pan
✓ newspaper covered work area

Process

1. Place the blossom head of the sunflower on the table. The head contains all the seeds in a wonderful spiral pattern from the center with tiny seeds to the outer edge with large seeds.
2. Remove individual seeds from the head with fingers and place each one in the container.
3. Smooth the surface of the sand in the baking pan, pressing with both hands to pack the sand firmly.
4. Arrange the individual sunflower seeds on top of the sand in designs or patterns.
5. When complete, move the pan with the sunflower seed design outside and watch for birds, squirrels, or other wildlife to come and eat the seeds. (Also save some seeds to bake and munch for snacks.)

Variation

■ Place seeds in a paper bag that has been decorated with drawings and take outside to feed to the birds and squirrels. Toss the seeds here and there.

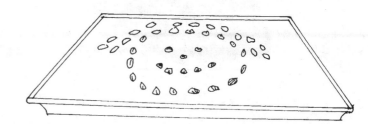

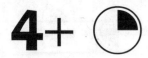
separation collage

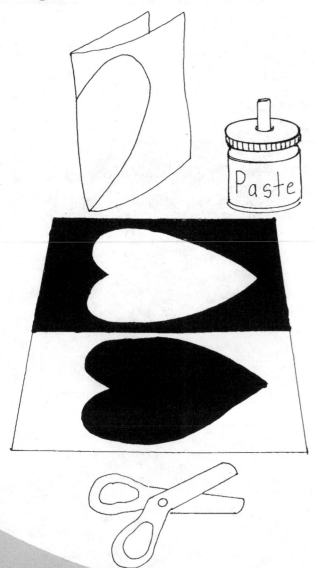

Positively Negative Illusion

Positive and negative shapes create interesting art and design contrasts that provide the artist with experiences with spatial relationships.

Materials
✓ black and white construction paper (or other contrasting colors), suggested approximate sizes: white paper 6" x 8", black paper 8" x 12"
✓ scissors
✓ pencil (optional)
✓ paste or white glue

Process
1. Fold a piece of white paper in half.
2. Cut a shape out of the folded side of the white paper. (It can be drawn first but that is not necessary. The shape will most often be abstract and unusual, but it can be a heart, rectangle, or other common shape.)
3. Unfold the cut-out piece. Unfold the white paper it was cut from too.
4. First paste the larger piece of white paper with the hole in it (the negative area) onto the black base paper, lining up the white paper along the edge and into the corner of the black paper (see illustration).
5. Next paste the piece cut from the white paper (the positive section) in the center of the remaining black paper (see illustration).

Variations
■ There are many variations and possibilities on this positive and negative design.
■ Instead of using construction paper, cut shapes from wrapping paper, fingerpaintings, or other designs and art projects that were created on paper and can be cut apart with the artist's permission.

122

Strips and Snips

Whole pieces of paper are cut or separated into strips and parts, but are brought back together in a new form using glue and tape—a way to explore separation.

separation collage

Materials

✓ construction paper in a variety of colors
✓ scissors (paper cutter for adult use)
✓ white glue or paste
✓ tape
✓ pinking shears (optional)
✓ drawing tools, such as
    crayons, markers, pencils

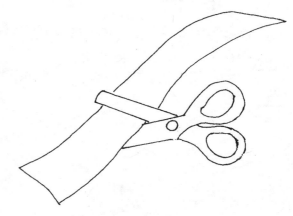

Process

1. Set aside a piece of colored paper as the background for Strips and Snips.
2. Cut construction paper into strips with scissors or pinking shears. (Adults can use a paper cutter to prepare strips ahead of time.)
3. Place whole strips of paper into a pile.
4. Cut smaller square and rectangular pieces from the strips.
5. Glue or paste a variety of strips of paper and snipped off pieces of strips in a sculpture, collage, or construction.
6. Further decorate the paper design with drawing materials, if desired.

Variations

■ Cut large freeform shapes from construction paper instead of strips.
■ Use pinking shears to cut strips.
■ Cut strips in wiggly or zigzaggy strips.

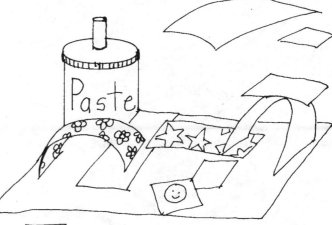

123

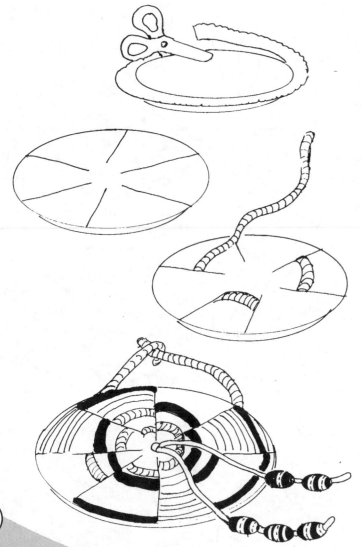

Weave Around the Circle

Weaving adds to the experience of exploring a whole paper plate circle that is separated into parts, and then rejoined by the weaving of yarn through those parts.

Materials
✓ heavy paper plate
✓ scissors
✓ multicolored, multitextured yarns
✓ beads
✓ markers or crayons (optional)

Process
1. Trim away the edge of the paper plate with scissors.
2. Cut slits toward the center, but not all the way through the plate.
3. Space the slits fairly evenly around the plate. Four to six slits is a good number.
4. Weave multicolored, multitextured yarn in and out of the slits. Make a few rows of weaving, or make many rows.
5. With adult help, use the scissors to poke a hole in the middle of the plate.
6. Tie pieces of yarn through the hole. Put beads on the ends of the yarn pieces that hang through the hole. Tie a knot to keep the beads from falling off, on the front and the back of the paper plate circle.
7. Add a loop of yarn for hanging the weaving.
8. Color the remaining white parts of the plate, if desired, with crayons or markers.

Variations
■ Cut small slits in the circle and weave yarns criss-crossing about from one slit to another like a spider web.
■ Add sewing trims or collage items to the yarn weaving.
■ Create a weaving on a square or any other shape of matte board.

Pizza Puzzle

Construct and decorate a pizza on a thin cardboard circle that can be divided to share, and then reassembled, as a way to explore the parts and the whole.

Materials

✓ pizza-sized circle cut from thin cardboard, paper plate, or recycled file folder
✓ scissors
✓ glue or tape
✓ red marker
✓ materials for creating toppings, such as magazine or catalog clippings, colored paper, stickers, collage materials, cut-out drawings of toppings
✓ pizza box or ziplock baggie for storing

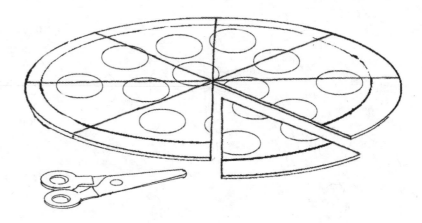

Process

1. With the red marker, color red pizza sauce on the cardboard circle.
2. Using materials of choice, cut and paste decorative toppings on the cardboard pizza circle. Some ideas for pizza toppings

bacon	meatballs	olives
cheese slices	mushrooms	pepperoni

3. When the glue is dry, cut the pizza circle into slices. Adult help may be needed if the cardboard circle base is thick.
4. A workable idea is to cut the pizza in half to begin. Then cut each half in half again. Further halving is up to the artist, but at least two to four pieces are needed. Note: Most artists cut the pizza into fairly equal triangle slices. Don't be surprised that some artists like to cut the pizza into many puzzle pieces.
5. Pretend to share the pizza slices with friends or toys. The pizza can be reassembled over and over.
6. Store the pieces in a plastic ziplock baggie or a clean pizza box.

Variations

■ Separate or cut into sections other foods to eat, such as an orange, apple, cake, brownies, or sandwich.
■ Slice a full loaf of bread into sections. Each artist can decorate a slice with a choice of jam, raisins, peanut butter, almond butter, or other yummy or decorative foods.
■ Draw a pie of any kind on paper, such as apple, cherry, or pumpkin. Cut out the pie, and then cut the whole pie into slices to play with and share.

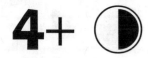
Spongy Cut-Ups

Used, dry commercial sponges in different colors are divided into parts and then stacked, explored, and eventually glued into a sponge sculpture.

Materials
✓ sponges in assorted colors
✓ scissors
✓ cardboard cut into 9" x 12"
✓ white glue
✓ food coloring in shallow dishes, full strength
✓ eyedropper for each dish of food coloring or liquid watercolors

Process
1. Place the different colors of commercial sponges on a table.
2. With scissors cut large sponges into smaller pieces. Sponges can sometimes be torn by hand.
3. Play, stack, and explore with sponge pieces.
4. When satisfied with exploring, arrange the pieces of sponge on the cardboard in a sculpture.
5. Glue into place and dry overnight.
6. When dry, sponges can be decorated with drops of food coloring or watercolors from an eyedropper.

Variations
■ Float and soak sponges in water in a plastic tub for a hot weather activity.
■ Use sponge pieces for making prints with ink, paint, or food coloring on paper or cardboard.

Layered Wiggle Art

Gelatin is a bright and delicious art medium to explore the qualities of sorting edible decorations, patterns in decorating, and division in servings.

Materials

✓ 2 or more boxes of gelatin mix, such as Jell-O, any flavors or colors
✓ boiling water and cold water (with adult supervision)
✓ measuring cups and spoons, pie pan
✓ knife or scissors
✓ refrigerator
✓ serving dishes, spoons, forks
✓ edible decorations, such as
    nuts, marshmallows (big and little), variety of fruits and vegetables, dried fruits, raisins

Process

1. Start by making a layer of gelatin in the pie pan. Follow the directions on the box with adult help.
2. Put the pan in the refrigerator until firm.
3. With the knife or scissors, cut and sort fruit, nuts, veggies, or other foods into pieces. Use caution or have adult help with the knife.
4. Make a design or pattern on the layer of gelatin with the food pieces. Some suggestions are flowers, scenes, abstract designs, letters, shapes, birds, silly critters.
5. Mix about one-half a box of gelatin with one-half the amount of water for the full box.
6. Spoon this gelatin gently over the design in the pan. Cover each piece (but don't use too much gelatin or the pieces will not stay put and will float instead).
7. Now, back goes the artful gelatin into the refrigerator for at least one hour.
8. Repeat another layer of gelatin. Add more foods such as raisins. Back to the refrigerator again. Repeat as many layers as desired, changing flavors and colors for each layer or staying with one flavor.
9. When it's time to eat the Layered Wiggle Art, cut it in wedges or squares and serve while still cold and firm. Mmmm, delicious and creative!

(127)

4+

**division
collage**

Colored Glue Creations

When shapes formed by the glue are cut into pieces and then glued on a base background paper, the artist experiences division.

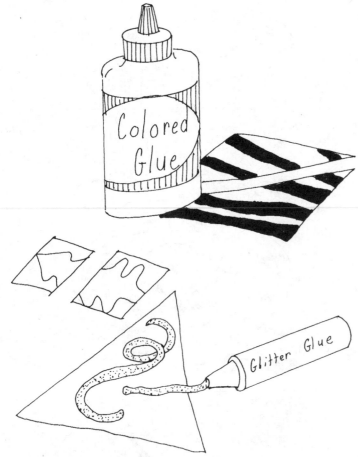

Materials
✓ plain paper
✓ scissors
✓ bottles of colored glue in several colors (available in school supply sections of most stores)
✓ colored glitter-glue (optional, white glue can be tinted with food coloring or paint)
✓ paper, matte board, or other background
✓ paste or white glue (can first be colored with tempera paint or food coloring)

Process
1. Cut paper into shapes such as triangles, rectangles, circles, or other abstract or unique shapes. Adult help may be needed.
2. Draw a glue design on each shape using colored glue or colored glitter-glue.
3. Allow colored glue shapes to dry.
4. Cut some, but not all, of the shapes apart like puzzle pieces.
5. Paste or glue assorted colored glue shapes and their parts on matte board, paper, or another background. Glue some of the whole shapes to the collage too.

Variations
■ Use colored glue on fluorescent board or cardboard pieces.
■ Use glitter pens or glitter with white glue.
■ Paint the shapes and sprinkle with glitter, colored sand, or confetti.
■ Make glue lines on the shapes. Then press them into a pan of salt. Next touch the salty glue gently with the tip of a dripping wet paintbrush filled with watercolor paint. Wow!

Exploring Spatial Relationships

PART 3

Look at Me Go...
Exploring Number Value

CHAPTER 7

Really Counting

Math concepts explored in this chapter

Counting
Number Value
Making Numerals

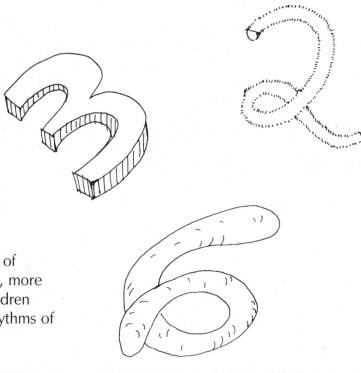

Understanding numbers begins early in life. Toddlers show a sense of knowing about more than one when they ask for another cookie, more banana, or just as many M&M's as their older brother. Older children may hear "chains of numbers" when they hear rhymes and singsong rhythms of numbers in games such as hide-and-seek or jump rope.

Integrated learning of the meaning of numbers occurs when a child begins to count objects. Understanding the idea of one object having one number, or 1-to-1 correspondence, is significant to early counting. Young learners will make natural developmental errors when learning to count, such as starting to count before touching the object to be counted, skipping a number when counting in sequence, or counting an object more than once.

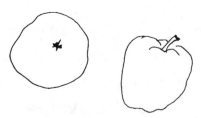

Working with countable materials helps children learn the process of counting. When children practice counting objects such as cotton balls, jar lid magnets, or fingers and toes, the representation of that number and number value can be understood. For example, the numeral 10 can represent ten fingers, ten toes, or ten apples; the numeral 3 can represent a Mom, Dad, and child.

While working with bright paints, yarn, sand, coffee grounds, and cupcake cups in the mathart activities in this chapter, children will have experiences that develop the math skills of counting and numeral recognition as well as actually forming numerals with art materials. This is a gradual developmental process for children to understand number quantity, symbolic representation, and relationships. Through exploration and discovery, through hands-on mathart experiences, and through experimenting with materials, the young learner will come to understand symbolic representation, that is, numeral recognition.

Exploring Number Value

Ten Little Fingers Design

By using prints of fingers or toes in an art design, young learners explore their most reliable and accessible counting materials—their own fingers and toes.

Materials
✓ fingers and toes (hands or feet)
✓ ink pad
✓ paper
✓ paper scraps
✓ scissors
✓ white glue
✓ crayons, markers, paints and brushes
✓ towels to clean fingers and toes

Process

1. Decide to make prints from either fingers or toes. Fingers are the easiest to start with but either choice is fun.
2. Press fingertips, all five from one hand, on the ink pad. Then press them on a sheet of paper, making a print of five fingertips all at once.
3. Repeat the printing of fingertips with the other hand. Now there should be ten dots or fingerprints on the paper.
4. The rest of the activity is freeform, although a few suggestions are given below:
    Cut, paste, glue, draw, and decorate the ten fingerprints.
    Draw details to make the ten prints into ten little creatures, bugs, or animals.
    The prints could be parts of flowers created from paper scraps and glued on.
    Red fingerprints could be berries or cherries.
    First draw branches and the fingerprints can be pussy willows.
    Number the fingerprints with bright colored crayons from one to ten.

Variation

■ For one-to-one correspondence, press a fingerprint on sticky-dots that are stuck to a piece of paper. Press one fingerprint in each colorful dot. Add string pieces and glue to make them look like balloons, if desired.

(133)

counting
printing

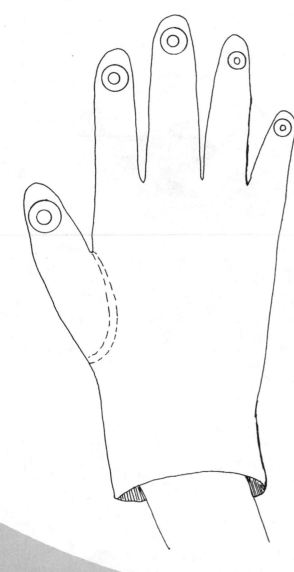

Hand in Glove Counting Prints

Adhesive corn pads seem a little silly to most children, but when used in this activity, these stick-ons take on new artistic meaning and value.

Materials
✓ latex surgical gloves
✓ rubber band (optional)
✓ small adhesive pads, such as corn pads, at least 5
✓ tempera paint in a cup or dish
✓ paintbrush
✓ paper
✓ soapy bucket of warm water, towels
✓ clothesline with clothespins

Process
1. Slip the glove on over all five fingers and hand. If desired, secure the glove to the wrist with a rubber band but not too tight.
2. Stick a corn pad on the printing side of each finger on the glove.
3. With a paintbrush paint the pads of the glove with the free hand. It's fine to paint the glove.
4. Press the painted glove and pads on the paper firmly and lift. Count the number of fingers and corn pads. There should be five of each! One, Two, Three, Four, Five.
5. Continue to make prints, over and over. Count all the fingers and pad prints.
6. When complete, wash glove and hands in the soapy bucket of water. Dry with old towels. Hang up the gloves to dry on a clothesline. Use again.
7. Prints may also dry on the clothesline.

Variations
■ On the thumb, stick one pad. On the pointer, stick two pads. On each finger in line, press three, four, or five pads. If pads are too big, cut them in pieces. Make prints.
■ Press one bunion pad on the thumb. Cut another bunion pad in half and press the two pieces on the pointer. Cut another pad in three pieces for the third finger, four pieces for the fourth, and five pieces for the fifth. Make prints.

Squished Clay Counters

   5+

There are many wonderful objects to collect and use as counters for sorting and counting. Even more fun is creating original counting items from clay.

Materials

✓ modeling clay, such as Fimo
✓ covered work area
✓ oven preheated to 275°F
✓ glass baking pan

Process

Simple Clay Counters (See Variations for other ideas.)
1. Pinch off small marble-size bits of clay from the modeling clay block.
2. Roll the bits into balls, about the size of small marbles.
3. Place a clay ball on the table and flatten and squish it with the palm of the hand.
4. Place the squished counters on the glass baking pan. Bake for 5 minutes.
5. With adult help, remove from the pan and let cool. Use as countable items.

Variations

■ **Big Clay Print Counters**
   Make a larger marble-size ball of modeling clay. Place on a sheet of wax paper. Flatten the ball into a circle. Then place a flat object (paper clip, coin, button) face down on the clay to make an impression or imprint. Cover with another piece of wax paper. Roll over it with a rolling pin. Remove carefully. Place the object on a glass pan and bake for about 15 minutes. Cool.

■ **Squished Bug Counters**
   Start with a medium marble-size ball of clay. Add designs and features to the ball such as eyes, nose, mouth, and hair. Then, take a flat object like a block and smash the ball. The result is a squished bug! Bake for 5 to 10 minutes on a glass pan. Cool.

■ **Moon and Star Counters**
   Roll a piece of clay out flat. Cut little stars, moons, circles, or other shapes from the flattened clay, just like making cookies but smaller. Remove the clay from around the shapes. Bake and cool.

■ **Jelly Roll Counters**
   Roll out two rectangles of clay in contrasting colors, but roll them to be the same size. Trim if necessary. Place one color on top of the other color. Roll the two pieces up together into a log. Roll the log a little more by hand to smooth it out. Chill in the refrigerator. Slice the chilled clay log into pieces. Bake the pieces on a glass pan for 10 minutes. (Use adult help with the sharp knife and baking.) Cool and count.

(135)

counting collage

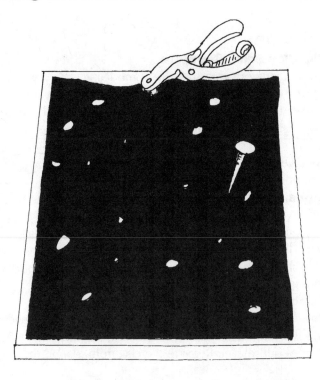

Bright Lights

Colored art tissue paper or bright cellophane combined with black paper and bright lights makes a beautiful display for artists learning to count.

Materials
✓ black paper or matte board
✓ heavy cardboard for work surface
✓ poking tools (with adult help) such as
    pencil, nail, pin, bamboo skewer, scissors, hole punch
✓ tape, white glue
✓ scraps of colored art tissue and bright cellophane

Process
1. Place a square of black paper or the piece of matte board on the cardboard work surface.
2. Use the poking tools to puncture holes in the black paper. Make as many holes as can be counted easily. For example, poke eight holes if that is a comfortable number to count to. Some artists will count one or two, others will count twenty or more. Some artists will count, "One, and one, and one . . ."
   Hint: Larger holes can be cut with scissors by sticking the tips into one of the poked holes and then gently snipping with little snips to start a bigger hole. A hole punch will work around the edges but doesn't reach in far enough to punch holes in the middle.
3. Poke, punch and cut as many holes as desired, then turn the black paper over. Tape or glue pieces of colored art tissue or cellophane over the holes. One large piece could cover the whole design, or many smaller pieces could be individually placed over each hole.
4. Hold the Bright Lights design up to a window or light fixture. Count or enjoy the colors and design.
5. Bright Lights can be displayed in a window for many artists to enjoy and count.

Variations
■ Work on a black paper that has been cut into the shape of a numeral. Then poke that many holes into the shape, covering the holes with pretty colors of paper.
■ Poke holes in colored paper and tape the paper to a sheet of black paper which makes the holes seem to pop out.

Exploring Number Value

Blossom Rolls

 5+

This activity is simply the experience of manipulating 100 objects and seeing the patterns that emerge. If 100 seems too many, use fewer items, such as 5, 10, 20, or 50.

Materials
- ✓ collect 100 cardboard tubes
- ✓ white photocopy or typing paper
- ✓ large piece of cardboard
- ✓ scissors
- ✓ tape
- ✓ white glue
- ✓ paper clips
- ✓ watercolor paints, brushes, jars of water
- ✓ colorful art tissue

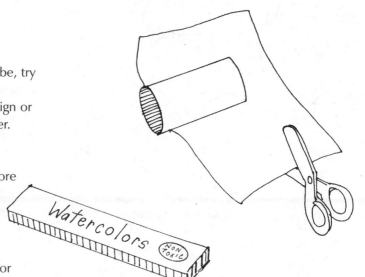

Process
1. To begin, roll a sheet of white paper around each tube. If the paper is bigger than the tube, try tucking or stuffing the extra into the tube or cut it away with scissors.
2. Glue paper tubes on the sheet of cardboard so the tubes are standing on end in any design or pattern. Glue the ends to the cardboard and also glue the sides of the tubes to each other.
3. Secure the tubes side to side with paper clips, if desired.
4. With watercolor paints, paint the white paper tubes with colors, lines, patterns, designs.
5. When the painting is complete, stuff fluffy squares of colorful art tissues in each tube. More than one color can be stuffed in each tube.
6. Observe what 100 (or how ever many were chosen) bright tube blossoms look like.

Variations
- Create a collage with 100 paper towel tubes, yogurt cups, empty plastic deli containers, or paper cups.
- Create one Blossom Rolls Collage with 10 tubes. On a cardboard next to the first, create one with 20 tubes. On the next cardboard, one with 30, next 40, next 50, and so on, so artists can visualize and experience the progression from 10 to 100.

(137)

Cupcake Garden

Children who can count will be able to design flowers with counted parts, petals, and leaves. Those who are not yet counting will explore one-to-one correspondence.

Materials
✓ paper cupcake cups
✓ white glue
✓ counting collage items, such as
      popcorn kernels, cotton balls, popped popcorn, colored circle stickers, beads
✓ sheet of butcher paper
✓ construction paper scraps
✓ scissors
✓ crayons

Process
For children who are learning to count
1. Follow the project below, but place only one collage item inside each flower cup. Then decorate the flower in any design.

For children who can count
1. Glue a cupcake paper cup to the sheet of paper.
2. Think of a number, for example, 3.
3. Count three collage items and glue them in the cup.
4. Cut three scraps from the construction paper and glue them like petals for a flower around the cup. Coloring petals is an alternative to cutting and pasting them.
5. If desired, cut three leaves and glue them to the flower too. Coloring leaves is another choice.
6. Add more flowers to the garden for any selected number to count, or as high as counting is possible.
7. Add grass, clouds, birds, bees, or other details for completing the garden.

Variation
■ Start with one collage item in the first flower of 10 total flowers, and count out collage items for each flower all the way to 10 on a long sheet of butcher paper. One in the first flower cup, two in the second, three, four, and so on.

Exploring Number Value

Glitter Rock Counting Collage

  5+

Most children seem to love rocks, pebbles, and gravel. Little stones become lovely, glittering treasures to count and enjoy in a lasting display.

Materials
✓ pressed paper apple divider (looks a bit like a paper muffin pan)
✓ tempera paints, several colors
✓ paintbrushes
✓ disposable containers for paint mixtures, 1 for each color, such as
   small milk cartons, yogurt cups, cottage cheese tubs
✓ white glue
✓ small rocks and stones, clean and dry
✓ colored glitter-glue in squeeze bottles
✓ newspaper-covered work area

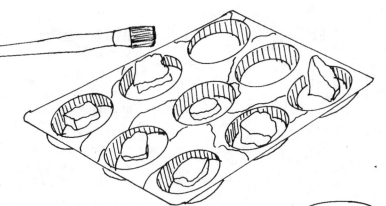

Process
1. Mix paint with glue, about half and half, in disposable containers.
2. Mix a different color in each container. Stir the mixture with a paintbrush and leave that brush in the container as the painting tool.
3. Paint the apple divider with the paint and glue mixture. Paint each section a different color, or mix colors in any pattern desired. Dry.
4. In one of the sections, glue one rock. In another section, glue two rocks. In another, three rocks, and so on. Glue as many rocks as can be counted.
   Note: Some artists who can count to one will glue one rock in each section, thereby having many sections with only one rock each. Others who can count five rocks can glue one, two, three, four, and five rocks in each section.
5. Dry. Then, take glitter-glue and squeeze sticky sparkles on the rocks. Some artists will develop a pattern, such as sections of five rocks are blue, sections of three rocks are red and so on. Other artists will work randomly. Dry completely until shiny and sparkly.

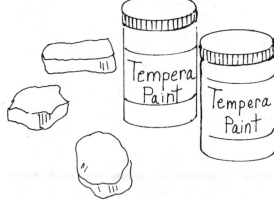

Variation
■ Imagine the different results from different collage items to count!
   buttons, handmade beads, feathers, shells, nuts and bolts, jewelry parts,
   handmade counters, small toys, drawings, photos

139

5+

counting craft

Jar Lid Magnets

There is no expectation for young children to count to 100; this activity is simply the experience of creating and manipulating 100 objects and seeing the patterns that emerge.

Materials
✓ 100 baby food jar lids
✓ crayons
✓ markers
✓ old magazines
✓ pencil
✓ scissors
✓ white glue or tape
✓ adhesive magnetic strips
✓ cookie sheet
✓ metallic display board or refrigerator door

Process
1. Collect 100 baby food jar lids. (If the artist can't count to 100, choose a number that is in the counting ability of that child, but working with 100 is fun even if the artist can't count that high.)
2. Create an "artwork" to glue inside the jar lid. Some suggestions are:
   Trace a lid on a section of a magazine picture.
   Trace a lid on a section of a fingerpainting.
   Trace a circle on plain paper and draw something in the circle.
   Trace a lid on a section of a piece of artwork or drawing.
   Trace a lid on a section of a greeting card, wrapping paper, or poster.
3. Cut out the circle. Glue it inside the lid. (A loop of tape on the back of the cut-out circle works well too.)
4. Create a total of 100 circles and glue them inside 100 total jar lids.
5. Stick a square of adhesive magnetic strip to the back of each jar lid.
6. Place all 100 lids on a magnetic surface such as a refrigerator door or a metallic display board.

(Continued on next page)

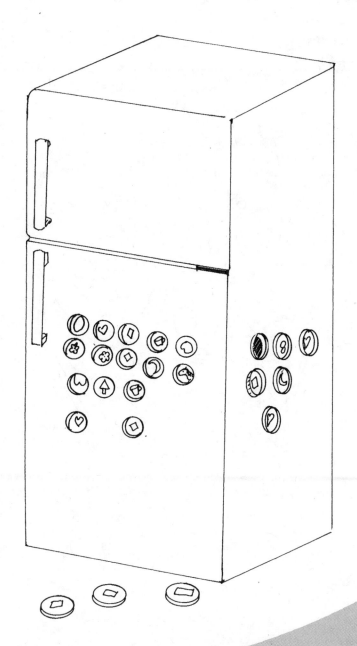

7. Group the 100 lids in designs. Some suggestions are:
        a square with 10 rows of 10
        pyramid shape, one at top, two next, and so on
        circles and flower shapes
        zigzags
As the artist groups and manipulates the lids, mathematical patterns will appear.

Variations

- Collect 100 caps from juice or soft drink bottles. Glue them in a pattern on a piece of heavy cardboard.
- Glue 100 craft sticks in a collage.
- Cut 100 paper shapes and glue in a collage.
- String 100 beads on a piece of yarn.
- Create a caterpillar made from 100 paper shape sections.

**counting
craft**

"How Old Am I" Hat

Making a special hat to announce a child's age creates a unique birthday hat that can be added to each year.

Materials
✓ any hat, old or new
✓ big buttons
✓ needle and thread
✓ fabric glue or craft glue
✓ hot glue gun with adult supervision (optional)
✓ felt
✓ scissors
✓ sewing trims, ribbons, beads, fabric scraps
✓ fabric paint (optional)

Process
1. Celebrate one birthday age, such as 5.
   Note: Create this hat a day before the birthday so it has time to dry.
2. Count and choose five fancy buttons from a box of buttons.
3. Sew or glue the buttons to the hat's brim or other prominent area.
4. Cut the numeral 5 out of felt.
5. Glue it to the hat in a place of honor with fabric glue (or a hot glue gun used by an adult).
6. Add additional trims, ribbons, or beads to the hat to make it unique and special.
7. Dry for several hours. Then wear to announce the age of the birthday child.

Variations
■ Create a special birthday shirt with the same materials.
■ Create a special birthday shirt with fabric crayons or paints.
■ Create a special birthday necklace with the correct number of birthday beads.

Exploring Number Value

Count Down Gift

Prepare a yummy munch mix by counting backward and measuring. Then place it in an originally decorated container for a unique gift.

Materials

- ✓ oven preheated to 350°F
- ✓ large wooden spoon
- ✓ airtight container
- ✓ old sponges
- ✓ styrofoam tray
- ✓ measuring cups and spoons
- ✓ large baking pan
- ✓ acrylic paint and paintbrush
- ✓ scissors

Process

Prepare the Count Down Munch Mix

1. Place the butter and brown sugar in the large baking pan, mixing them together thoroughly. Count down almonds and walnuts into the pan with the butter and sugar.
2. With adult help, place this mixture in the oven and bake for 5 minutes. Remove from the oven and stir.
3. Bake in the same pan for an additional 6 minutes. Remove, and cool for 5 minutes, all in the same pan.
4. Count down the remaining ingredients into the baking pan with the almonds, walnuts, sugar and butter. Stir and mix well.
   Note: Serves 6 to 10.
5. Store in an airtight container (the gift container).

Decorate the gift container

1. Spread acrylic paints in blobs on a clean styrofoam tray.
2. Cut an old sponge into shapes, such as numbers, letters, or simple shapes. Press a sponge shape into the paint and then print that shape on the plastic container.
3. Decorate the container in any way you wish. Then dry completely overnight.
4. The decorated container filled with Munch Mix is ready to give as a gift. When the munchies are gone, the container can still be enjoyed and used over and over.
   Note: The paints will eventually wash off the container.

Count Down Munch

Mix ingredients
1/4 cup butter, melted
1/3 cup firmly packed brown sugar

Count down with
10 tablespoons silvered almonds
9 tablespoons chopped walnuts
8 tablespoons raisins
7 tablespoons dried bananas
6 tablespoon semisweet chocolate chips
5 tablespoons shredded coconut
4 tablespoons sunflower seeds
3 tablespoons peanuts
2 tablespoons dried apricots
1 cup uncooked rolled oats
Serves 6 to 10

**number value
drawing**

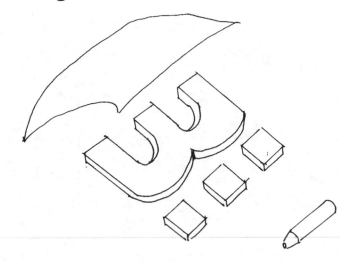

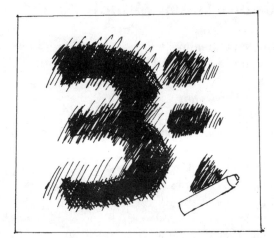

Numeral Rubbing Resist

Manipulating counting items helps the artist learn by experience how many items go with which numeral, a more difficult concept than counting alone or knowing the names of numerals alone.

Materials
✓ peeled crayons in a variety of colors
✓ numeral shapes, precut (with adult help) from heavy paper squares, about 3" x 3"
✓ yarn scraps
✓ flat collage materials for crayon rubbings, such as
      paper clips, bingo markers, paper scraps, rubber bands,
      coins, small tiles, leaves, buttons
✓ paper hole punches
✓ butcher paper or construction paper
✓ tempera paint thinned with water in a cup
✓ wide, soft paintbrush
✓ tape (optional)

Process
1. Choose a numeral shape, for example, 3. Place it on the table.
2. Count out three flat collage items and place near, under, around, or next to the paper numeral.
3. Cover the numeral and collage items with the bigger piece of paper. Tape the corners to prevent paper from wiggling, if desired.
4. Rub over the paper with a peeled crayon, hard and bright. Use several colors, if desired, exposing a rubbing of the numeral 3 and the three items.
5. When satisfied with the rubbing, paint over the rubbing with watery, thin tempera paint using a soft, wide brush. The paint will bead up and resist the wax crayon, and will adhere only to the uncolored paper.
6. When ready, move the rubbing resist to a drying area, and work on a new sheet of paper with a different numeral. Make as many as desired.

Variation
■ Use a long strip of paper and create a rubbing resist of numbers 1 through 10 in order.

Number Paintings

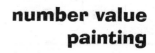

number value painting

When a young child first begins to recognize a number and also knows the value of that number, all kinds of new art possibilities open up, such as Number Paintings.

Materials
✓ paint easel
✓ 1 color paint and 1 brush, to begin (as many as 10 colors of paint and 10 brushes, later on)
✓ paper
✓ wide marker
✓ apron or shirt to cover artist

Process

To begin
1. An adult or the artist writes the numeral 1 on the paper at the easel. The numeral can be small in the corner, or large and cover most of the paper. The artist can direct how the numeral should be drawn and placed. One color of paint will be available.
2. With the one color of paint, paint on the paper. Some artists may choose to paint one shape; others will cover the paper in one color; others will paint the numeral 1. The results are open. The main idea is that the numeral 1 on the paper tells how many colors should be used.

To progress
1. Write a numeral such as 2, 3, or 4 on the easel paper. Have two, three, or four colors of paint available.
2. The artist paints with as many colors as the numeral directs. The artist may also choose her own numeral, write it on the paper, and paint with that many colors.
   Note: Many artists will incorporate the numeral into the design; others will completely cover it in paint; others will ignore its presence.

Variation
■ Select a numeral, such as 4, to direct the painting: have four colors of paint, four colors of crayon, four collage items, four colors of art tissue, and so on. The artist can incorporate four of everything she wishes in the Number 4 Painting.

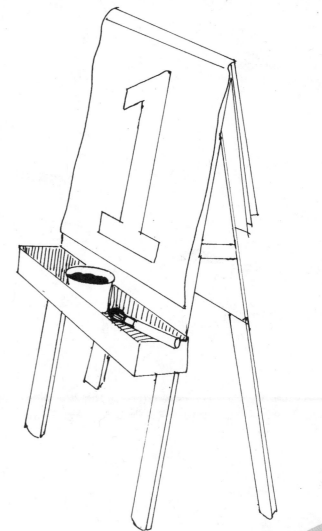

145

5+

number value
clay

Candy Clay Count

A yummy way for children to learn about number value, measuring, and number order is creating edible candy counters. A great birthday party decoration!

Materials
✓ 1/3 cup butter
✓ 1/3 cup light corn syrup
✓ 1/2 teaspoon salt
✓ 1 teaspoon vanilla
✓ 1 pound box powdered sugar
✓ food coloring or paste coloring
✓ bowl
✓ small bowls or cups for different colors
✓ spoon
✓ 10 small paper plates

Process
1. Wash and dry hands.
2. Blend the first four ingredients, and then mix in the powdered sugar. Knead by hand until smooth. Add more powdered sugar if necessary.
3. Separate the white clay into several different cups, one for each color you choose. Drop several drops of food coloring into each cup or add food paste to each cup. Mix by hand or with a spoon. Wash hands between color mixing.
   Note: Paste food coloring gives Candy Clay bright, amazing hues.
4. Pinch off some clay and form the numeral 1. Place it on the first plate. Pinch off more clay and form the numeral 2. Place it on the second paper plate. Make all numerals from 1 to 10 and place them in order, one on each plate.
5. Now add more clay decorations to each numeral such as dots, stripes, flowers, and so on.
6. To decorate the numbers to show their value, place one decoration on the 1, two on the 2, three on the 3, and so on.
7. The Candy Clay display can be eaten as is, or used to decorate cupcakes, graham crackers, or cookies.

Cotton Ball Secret Sculpture

The secret number the artist selects for this project determines the design and creative approach.

Materials
✓ shoe box
✓ colorful modeling clay or play dough
✓ construction paper
✓ white glue
✓ scissors
✓ collage items
✓ cotton balls
✓ newspaper-covered work area

Process
1. Stand a shoe box on its side so it looks like an open stage.
2. Line the box in any fashion with construction paper and glue, if desired.
3. Meanwhile, think of a secret number from 1 to 10 that will determine the number of cotton balls in the shoe box. For example, use the number 5.
4. Begin building a scene in the box with clay and other collage items.
5. Incorporate five cotton balls into the design, but don't tell anyone how many cotton balls there are in the design.
6. When complete, other artists can guess and count how many cotton balls they can find in the Cotton Ball Secret Sculptures.

Variations
■ Select a secret number, for example, 2. Everything in the design should be in twos: two flowers, two baskets, two trees, two birds, and so on.
■ Substitute a different collage item instead of the cotton balls to designate the secret number. For example, if the number is 3, there could be three beads, three buttons, three pipe cleaners, and so on.

147

**number value
assemblage**

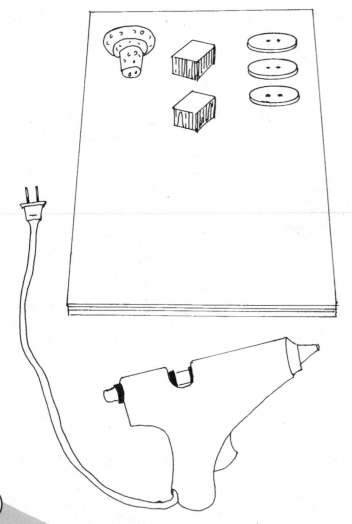

Counting Board

When a young learner creates a counting board, she counts out interesting art materials and assembles them in an artistic design.

Materials
✓ piece of plywood
✓ hammer and nails
✓ white glue (or hot glue gun with adult assistance)
✓ items for the counting assemblage, such as
　　　corks, blocks of wood, nuts, bolt, nails, hardware items, aluminum foil,
　　　wooden or styrofoam spools, whatever collage items or odds and ends are on hand

Process
1. Spread out the materials for the assemblage so they are readily visible.
2. Choose one of an item, such as one cork, and attach it to the plywood with glue or a hammer and nail.
3. Next, choose two of something, such as two blocks of wood, and attach them to the plywood.
4. Continue, with three items, four items, five items, and so on.
5. Fill the board as desired, making patterns or groupings of any kind.
6. Dry completely.
7. When complete, look through the counting board and try to see how many of each item there are.

Variations
■ Instead of counting in order, the counting board could be a way to highlight one number and its value; that is, fill the board with one of each item, or two of each item, or three, or four, or whatever the chosen number is. For example, if two is the chosen number, fill the board with two corks, two pine cones, two beads, two of anything.
■ Create a Sticker Counting Board on a piece of matte board with stickers, labels, or sticky-dots.
■ Add written numerals to the assemblage.
■ Add clay or dough numerals to the assemblage.

Numeral Draw

Tactile experiences help the child learn more than just the way a numeral looks; the young learner experiences the way the numeral feels and how it is shaped.

Materials

✓ shallow baking pans
✓ any of the following loose materials, such as
    flour
    sand
    rice
    used, dried coffee grounds

Process

1. Fill shallow pans with one of the loose materials such as rice or sand.
2. Smooth, pat, and flatten the material with the hands.
3. Draw numerals in material with a finger or several fingers.
4. Draw and add other designs around the numerals.
5. To form new designs and numerals on a "clean slate," gently shake the pan back and forth, and then pat the sand or flour in the pan again. Draw again.
6. When drawing and exploring are complete, pour the flour or sand into a plastic bag and save to use for other projects.

Variations

■ Draw numerals in a sand table or sandbox.
■ Draw with other tools instead of fingers, such as
    popsicle stick, paintbrush, fork, comb, cotton swab, eraser, or pencil
■ Add other design features to the sand drawing, such as
    pieces of glitter, toys, colored sand,
    beads, paper bits

149

5+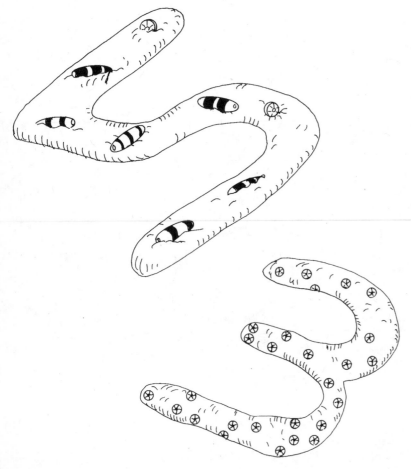

making numerals clay

Play Clay Favorite Numerals

When a child feels the shapes of numerals as he sculpts them from clay, he is more likely to remember them.

Materials
✓ clay or dough that dries hard (see page 47)
✓ decorative items, such as
      sequins
      beads
✓ food coloring or tempera paints
✓ eyedropper
✓ newspaper-covered work area

Process
1. Choose a numeral or series of numerals with meaning, such as a birthday or address.
2. Select a ball of clay and squeeze a few drops of food coloring or paint on the clay. Knead the color into the clay on a covered work area.
3. Model the clay into the special chosen numerals.
4. While the modeling clay is still wet, press decorative materials into the numeral to make imprints. The items can be counted to match the value of the number, or the items can simply be decorative.
5. Dry for 24 hours for regular size numerals, or longer for larger numerals.
6. Display the numerals to enjoy as they are or combine them with other materials in a collage or sculpture activity.

Variations
■ Instead of coloring the clay, paint the finished uncolored numerals. Then dry.
■ Create a sequential display of numerals from 1 to 10, each numeral with counted items pressed into it.

Exploring Number Value

Bread Dough Numerals

This delicious dough is very workable for sculpting numerals and other shapes that can then be eaten as part of a meal or for a snack.

Materials

- ✓ clean hands
- ✓ apron
- ✓ 1½ cups warm water
- ✓ large bowl
- ✓ 1 pkg. yeast
- ✓ 1 teaspoon salt
- ✓ 1 tablespoon sugar
- ✓ 4 cups flour

- ✓ floured surface
- ✓ greased cookie sheet
- ✓ towel
- ✓ warm spot for raising dough
- ✓ 1 egg, beaten
- ✓ pastry brush
- ✓ salt to taste (optional)
- ✓ honey, butter, jam, peanut butter

Process

1. With adult help, measure 1½ cups warm water into the large bowl. Sprinkle yeast into the water and mix until soft.
2. Add salt, sugar, and flour. Mix until dough forms a ball.
3. Knead on a floured surface until smooth and elastic.
4. Roll and twist the dough into numerals. Create other shapes too.
5. Place the bread dough sculptures on a greased cookie sheet.
6. Cover with a towel and let them rise in a warm place until double in size.
7. Brush each sculpture with beaten egg. Sprinkle with salt, if desired.
8. Bake for 12–15 minutes at 350°F until numeral sculptures are firm and golden brown. They should sound hollow when tapped with a knife.
9. Cool slightly. Eat and enjoy plain or with honey, jam, peanut butter, or other spreads.

Variations

- Bake a loaf of bread. When done, count the number of hungry people and slice the bread into that many sections.
- Attach balls of dough to the numerals to indicate their values. Bake. For example, attach three balls of dough to the numeral 3, 5 balls to the 5 and so on.

How Many Is Many?

Math concepts explored in this chapter

Measuring   **Weighing**
Estimating   **Graphing**
Time

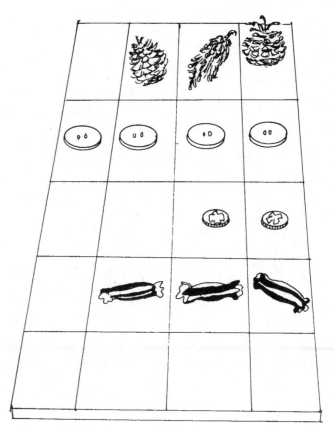

When young learners have had significant concrete and hands-on experiences such as those found throughout this book, they may be ready to understand concepts represented in symbolic form, such as the symbols on a clock or the numbers on a dollar bill. Graphing is one way for children to see counting, sorting, and comparing displayed visually. Guessing, estimating, and developing problem solving skills begin to take place as does reaching their own conclusions. There is no hurry to begin adding, subtracting, multiplying, or dividing, but many children will fall into them naturally because of their rich background in mathart integrated experiences.

Chapter 8 has a wide variety of mathart experiences that build on the concrete experiences from throughout this entire book, using materials such as handmade clay counters, to explore the concepts of measuring, weighing, estimating, graphing, and time.

Ruler Draw

Young artists can measure with a ruler using the straight edge to create an unusual abstract line design without actually knowing much about measurement, rulers, or number value. Working with a measuring tool like a ruler in an exploratory mode helps the child begin to learn the mathematical concept of measurement.

Materials

✓ ruler (6" ruler works well)
✓ sticker (optional)
✓ paintbrush

✓ pencil or markers
✓ crayons or watercolor paint
✓ white or light colored paper

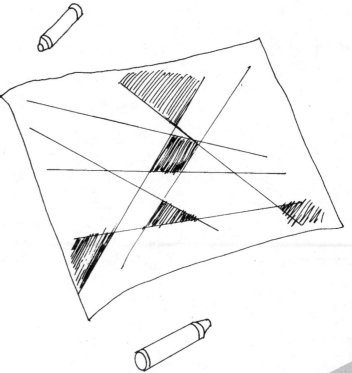

Process

1. Choose a point on the ruler that will determine the design, such as the numeral 5.
2. Mark the numeral with a dot, pen line, marker, or sticker. Place another mark or sticker at the beginning of the ruler too.
3. Place the ruler on the paper, holding it with one hand, and draw a line from the beginning of the ruler all the way to the marked numeral. Stop at the numeral.
4. Move the ruler to another part of the paper, perhaps intersecting or joining the first line. Draw another line from the beginning to the 5 or whatever numeral is chosen.
5. Continue moving the ruler and marking lines that are all the same length.
6. Draw lines until the paper is substantially filled with lines all the same length and the design feels comfortable.
7. With either crayons, watercolor paints, or both, fill in the spaces between the lines with color and patterns of any kind. If paint was used, let the design dry.

Variations

■ Incorporate the chosen numeral into the design. Take crayon and make 5s in the spaces created by the ruler and lines 5" long (or, again, whatever numeral was chosen).
■ For an easier version of the above, follow the same general directions for this project, but use a stiff piece of cardboard instead of a ruler. Make all the lines the length of the piece of cardboard.

155

5+ ◐

**measuring
painting**

Spoonful of Sugar

Measuring by spoonfuls is traditionally associated with cooking. But in this mathart activity, each spoonful of sugar helps the wet chalk dry glossy and less dusty. Measuring is an important part of preparing for the art experience and is easy for young children to do on their own.

Materials

- ✓ colored chalk, 3 colors
- ✓ flat rock or rolling pin
- ✓ wax paper
- ✓ 6 custard cups
- ✓ teaspoons
- ✓ bowl of sugar
- ✓ dish of white glue
- ✓ 3 paintbrushes
- ✓ paper
- ✓ small bucket of warm soapy water, towel

Process

1. Crush colored chalk with a flat rock or rolling pin on a sheet of wax paper. There is no need to pound, just press and roll back and forth firmly but gently.
2. Fold the wax paper and pour the chalk dust into a small dish or custard cup. Do the same for a total of three colors of crushed chalk in three custard cups.
3. Scoop up one rounded teaspoon of one color of crushed chalk from one of the cups and empty it into a clean custard cup.
4. Rinse and dry the spoon or use a different one. Scoop one teaspoon of sugar and empty it into the cup with the teaspoon of chalk. Stir gently.
5. Add one teaspoon of white glue. Be prepared for drips and runs. Stir the glue, chalk, and sugar together with a spoon or with one of the paintbrushes until mixed.
6. Now repeat the above steps for two more colors and cups of chalk, sugar, and glue.
7. When three (or more!) colors are prepared, dip a paintbrush into the mixture and paint with it on paper. Use a separate brush for each color, if you wish, or go ahead and use one brush for all colors, mixing and messing about.
   Note: When the chalk-sugar-glue painting dries, it will be glossy and crisp. Let it dry at least overnight or for several days for the glue to turn clear.

Variation

- Mix different colors of crushed chalk together to create new colors before adding the glue.

OneOneOne Dough Drop Design

Measure one cup each of flour, salt, and water to make the paint dough. Then squeeze "one drop dots" of dough from the container to create the design.

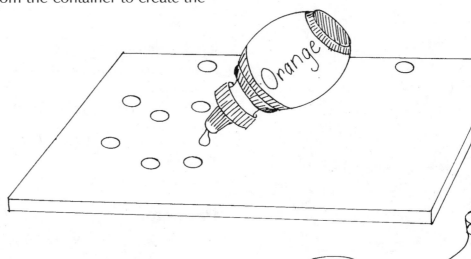

Materials

- ✓ tempera paint, several colors, liquid or powdered
- ✓ 1 cup flour for each color of paint
- ✓ 1 cup salt for each color of paint
- ✓ 1 cup water for each color of paint
- ✓ bowls, 1 for each color of paint
- ✓ several 1 cup measuring cups
- ✓ stick, spoon, or brush for stirring mixture
- ✓ spatula
- ✓ plastic squeeze bottles, 1 for each color of paint
- ✓ dough
- ✓ matte board

Process

1. The artist measures one cup each of flour, salt, and water in a bowl. Add just enough paint, liquid or powdered, to color the mixture to the desired intensity.
2. An adult can scrape the bowl with a spatula and fill a plastic squeeze bottle with the thick colored dough.
3. Meanwhile, prepare and mix two more colors of OneOneOne Dough Drop, each in a separate bowl. Fill two more squeeze bottles. Make more colors and fill more bottles, if desired.
4. Place the matte board on the table.
5. Squeeze one drop of dough on the matte board. (For this project, try for drops of dough that are all the same measurement or size instead of lines or other shapes.)
6. Change colors and fill the matte board with dough drops in many colors. Let the design dry overnight to a crystallized, rock hard, bright paint dough design.

157

5+ ◑

**measuring
sculpture**

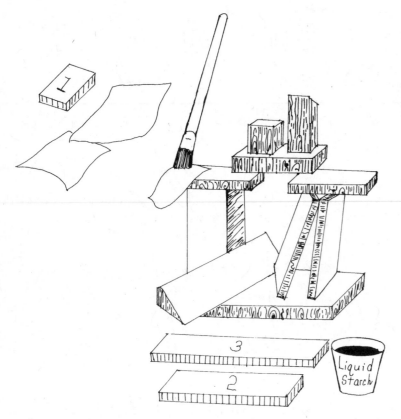

Block Measurement Sculpture

Sorting and measuring scraps of wood is challenging but appealing. The measuring and comparing activity (work!) prepares the materials for the art activity—building a wooden block sculpture and then decorating it with bright colors of art tissue.

Materials
✓ small framing scraps and blocks of wood scraps
✓ 3 strips of scrap cardboard, cut in the following lengths: 1", 2", and 3"
✓ white glue (adult supervised hot glue gun is a quick alternative)
✓ matte board, heavy cardboard, or flat piece of wood
✓ art tissue scraps and pieces
✓ paintbrush
✓ liquid starch in a cup

Process
1. First sort the blocks and scraps into three piles of those that are similar in length. Some artists will say, "Big ones, not so big ones, and littler ones."
2. From these three piles, use the cardboard "measuring scraps" to compare to the wood scraps. Select those scraps that compare (and measure) approximately 1", 2", or 3". Place these in three new piles to use for the art project. Put away the other pieces.
3. Starting with the 3" scraps first, glue them in any design on the matte board, beginning to build a sculpture. (An adult may assist with a hot glue gun.)
4. Next, glue on the 2" pieces, and lastly the 1" pieces, building the wood block sculpture in any three-dimensional design. Let the sculpture dry overnight.
5. The next day, spread a little liquid starch on one of the pieces of wood in the sculpture, and press a piece of colorful art tissue into the starched area. Then paint more starch on top of this. Cover a little or a lot of the sculpture with art tissue pieces and starch. The tissue pieces will "bleed" and stain the wood scraps, too.
6. Dry the sculpture until the tissue has a bit of a crunchy, parchment feeling. Paint more starch or white glue over the dry tissue for an extra layer of gloss, if desired.

Measure Me String Art

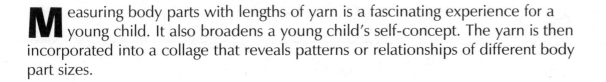

5+

Measuring body parts with lengths of yarn is a fascinating experience for a young child. It also broadens a young child's self-concept. The yarn is then incorporated into a collage that reveals patterns or relationships of different body part sizes.

Materials
- ✓ balls of yarn
- ✓ scissors
- ✓ tape (colored masking tape or craft tape is effective)
- ✓ white glue
- ✓ sheet of craft paper or poster board
- ✓ 2 children to work together (the measuring person and the measured person)

Process
1. Lay out the sheet of paper on the floor or tape it to the wall. The person measuring should pull out a piece of yarn and measure a part of the other person (the measured person), such as the length of an arm or leg. Snip the yarn at the measured length.
2. Tape or glue that piece of yarn to the craft paper. Stretching the yarn into a long, straight line is one way to do this.
3. Measure another part of the other person, such as around the head or a finger. Again, cut the yarn at the measured length and then tape or glue the yarn to the craft paper. One idea is to stretch the second piece of yarn next to the first, although crossing them over or joining them in a long design is artistically effective too.
4. Continue measuring with yarn until both artists are satisfied with the yarn display.
5. Trade places and now measure the other person on a fresh piece of craft paper, or use another color yarn and glue to the first person's paper.

Variations
- Look for comparisons between the yarn lengths. Sometimes there are patterns which are readily evident in lengths and parts of the body.
- Tape the yarn to a poster board—one piece of yarn next to the other—like a graph. Label the yarn pieces with a drawing of a foot, leg, neck, or another body part that was measured.

159

**measuring
construction**

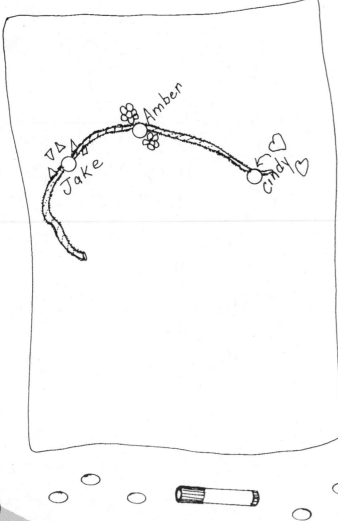

Heads Up Graph

Helping young children learn about their bodies encourages them to develop a positive self-concept. Measuring their height and making a graph of the measurement allows them to compare their heights to one another and to see their measurements graphically and artfully displayed.

Materials
✓ sticky-dots
✓ lightweight straight piece of wood (about 1' long)
✓ black marker
✓ yarn
✓ scissors
✓ tape, if needed
✓ strip of butcher paper taped horizontally to the wall at child height

Process
1. As one child stands with her back to the butcher paper, a friend places a sticky-dot on the paper even with her height. (Holding a lightweight piece of wood or book on top of her head will help show where the dot should go on the butcher paper. Some adult assistance may be needed.)
2. After the child steps away, she makes a design around the sticky-dot to identify the dot as hers. Writing a name works too.
3. Do the same for all the children in the group, spacing them about 1' to 2' apart on the paper. Each child will decorate her dot or write her name.
4. Take yarn and tape (or use a sticky-dot instead of tape) an end to the first sticky-dot measurement. Pull the yarn over to the next dot and tape it to that one. Then take it to each dot in order and tape it to the dot.
5. When the dots are connected from the first to the last, the yarn will go up and down with the different heights of the children. This will help them see the height measurements and how they compare graphically.
   Note: Sometimes children think tall is better than short, so watch for this and diffuse any competition or negative comparisons if they arise.
6. Further decorate the white areas above and below each sticky-dot with strips of colored paper, paint, aluminum foil, or sticky-dots in a row.

Little Stone Boxes

   5+

Stones of various weights are painted and placed in a sturdy, child-decorated box for play. The most basic scale of all—the sense of touch—is used to weigh the painted stones by hand, estimating or guessing.

Materials
✓ sturdy box with lid
✓ tempera paints and brushes
✓ smooth rocks and stones of various sizes
      heavy and light
      large and small
✓ fingernail polish
✓ non-acetone fingernail polish remover (adult assistance)

Process
1. Paint the box in any way with tempera paints. Dry completely.
2. Paint the smooth stones with fingernail polish. (When one side has dried, turn the stones over and paint the other side.)
3. While the stones are drying, an adult can help the artist clean away any fingernail polish from hands with non-acetone fingernail polish remover.
4. When all the stones are dried to a shiny hardness, handle the stones and feel the different weights and sizes. Notice the difference with eyes closed, too.
5. When satisfied with exploration of weights and sizes, place the stones in the decorated box for another day or another activity with weights or counting.

Variations
- Use glitter-glue and confetti to decorate the box.
- Paint the stones with a theme, such as happy faces, pumpkins, fruit, fish, stars, flowers.
- Use metallic paint to create gold or silver treasure stones.
- Use the painted stones for counting, sorting, patterns, or any activity in this book that needs objects that can be manipulated by small hands.

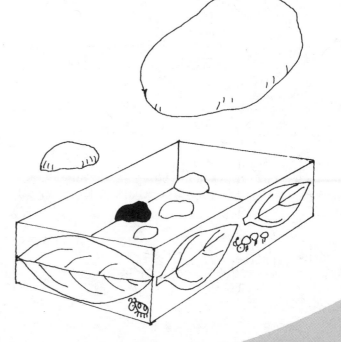

161

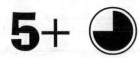

5+

**weighing
craft**

Surprise Egg

Commercial plastic Easter eggs are recycled and decorated into weighted objects and used in a weight and estimation activity. Young artists especially like experimenting by filling the eggs with different objects. There is a playful element of surprise in opening the eggs and rediscovering the contents.

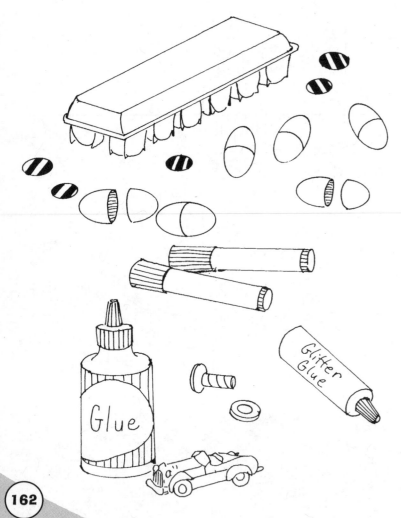

Materials

✓ egg carton
✓ permanent markers
✓ plastic Easter eggs (commercial type that open up and can be filled)
✓ glitter-glue
✓ fluorescent glue
✓ stickers, labels, sticky-dots
✓ small items of various weights to fill eggs such as
      feathers, nuts, screws, candy, washers, small cars,
      pennies, hardware items, painted pebbles, clay beads

Process

1. Decorate an egg carton with colored permanent markers. Set aside.
2. Open the plastic eggs and decorate the outside of each half with glue, stickers, and other materials. Dry completely.
3. When the eggs are dry, fill them with a selection of the small items of various weights. (Some artists may wish to work "secretly" so no one knows what is in the eggs.) Close the eggs.
4. Explore the feel of the different weights of the eggs. Try to guess what is inside by feeling the weight of each egg (a way of estimating).
5. Open the eggs and see how close each guess was.
6. Store eggs in the decorated egg carton.

Variation

■ Instead of plastic eggs, use small paper cups. Fill one cup with small items and then tape a second cup on top of the first, covering and sealing the seam with masking tape where the two cups join together. The cups will not come apart, but are used sealed together.

Hoop Mobile

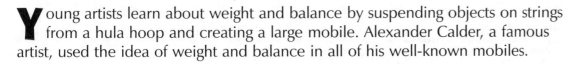 5+

Young artists learn about weight and balance by suspending objects on strings from a hula hoop and creating a large mobile. Alexander Calder, a famous artist, used the idea of weight and balance in all of his well-known mobiles.

Materials

✓ objects of various weights, such as
   pinecones, washers, cardboard tubes and shapes, small wood scraps, blocks, toy parts, rolled-up wallpaper, collage items, small books, paintbrushes, styrofoam shapes
✓ strong string
✓ masking tape or duct tape
✓ hula hoop

Process

1. Tie selected objects to strong string with a secure knot. Tie the string to the hula hoop, keeping the loop around the hoop slightly loose so adjustments for balance can be made. (See illustration.)
2. Slide and space the objects on the strings around the hoop.
3. An adult can add two longer pieces of string to the hoop for a hanger. Tie one string across the hoop (the piece should be longer than the distance across the hoop for slack). Then tie another string the same length the other way across the hoop so the two strings cross each other. Tie the two strings together with a loose loop of string where they cross.
4. Suspend the hoop mobile from its crossed string hanger at child height. Watch to see if the hoop is balanced. The heavier objects will tilt the hoop to one side and pull the mobile downward.
5. Adjust and balance the mobile by distributing the objects around the hoop, noting heavy and light objects that may need attention to aid in balancing the mobile.
6. When the mobile is balancing nicely, hang it higher from the ceiling so the air currents will make the objects sway and move.
7. The strings can be taped in place to prevent them from moving around the hoop.

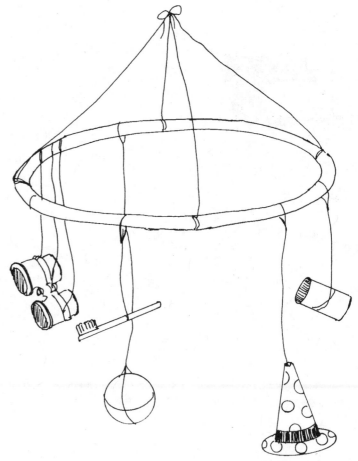

Variation

■ For the enjoyment of birds and animal friends, suspend treats from a tree branch, such as crackers spread with suet or peanut butter, stale bagels, sunflower head with seeds, paper cup filled with bird seed.

163

   (caution)

estimating clay

Beginner Buttons

Artists can make real buttons by rolling little balls of clay and flattening them by hand. Their senses of sight and touch will tell them if they are estimating in nearly equal or similar amounts.

Materials
✓ small marble-size balls of polymer modeling clay, such as Fimo
✓ toothpick
✓ glass baking pan
✓ oven preheated to 275°F

Process
1. Pinch off a piece of polymer modeling clay. Roll the clay into a small marble-size ball.
2. Pinch and roll one ball for each button to be made. Use one color or a variety of colors.
3. Flatten the ball by hand into a circle.
4. Use the toothpick to poke a pattern into the flattened circle, if desired.
5. Poke two holes with the toothpick to make a button. Place on the baking sheet.
6. Bake for 10 minutes at 275°F for small buttons, and 15 minutes for larger buttons. Cool.
7. Sew on a shirt, pillow, hat, or any article of clothing.
   Note: Clay buttons are fragile. Regular washing machines should be OK, but dry-cleaning will destroy them. Tumble drying is not recommended.

Variations
■ Mixed-color buttons are made by pinching off bits of a variety of colors of clay and rolling them together to form a small marble-size ball. Flatten the mixed-colored ball, poke button holes, and bake. Cool. Use as buttons.
■ Coiled buttons are made by rolling two clay ropes of contrasting colors and twisting them together. Coil the rope up like a cinnamon roll, flatten, poke holes, and then bake. Cool. Sew on clothing and use as real buttons.

Coiled Wire Jewelry

A stick of wood is the measuring tool; the artist estimates the lengths of the wire by comparing the wire to the stick.

Materials

✓ scrap wire
✓ scrap of wood about 6″ long, 1″ wide
✓ scissors and tape
✓ cylindrical block or pencil
✓ elastic cord

Process

1. A good source of scrap wire is colored wire from used telephone cable. Pipe cleaners also work well
2. Cut the wire to manageable lengths with scissors. (Help may be needed getting the wire ready.)
3. The artist stretches a piece of colored wire from one end of the 6″ wood scrap to the other, making a little bend in the wire to indicate the length and where to cut. Cut the wire on the bend mark. Set aside.
4. Repeat the stretching and cutting of another wire piece. Set aside.
5. Continue stretching and cutting wire until as many pieces as needed are set aside. About 10 or 20 pieces of wire work well, but even one piece is enough.
6. Wrap a piece of the cut wire around a cylindrical block or pencil. Wrap it fairly tight. Then slide the wrapped wire coil off of the block. It will keep its curled shape. Repeat the curling process for the rest of the wire scraps.
7. Next, tie the ends of the elastic cord together to form a circle big enough to stretch over the artist's head.
8. Take one of the curled wires and bend one end of it around the piece of elastic to attach the wire to the cord. Repeat this attaching step for as many curls as desired.
   Note: At this step, artists may wish to put their wire curls in a pattern or in some order. It is helpful, but not required, to line them up on the table in the order in which they are to be attached to the wire, and then begin attaching.
9. Wear and enjoy this curly, silly necklace!

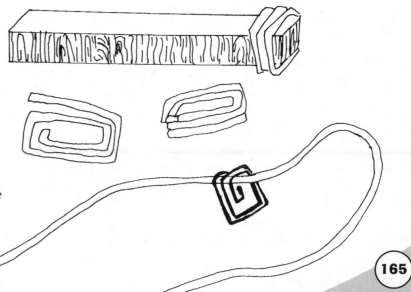

165

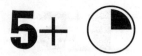

5+

**graphing
painting**

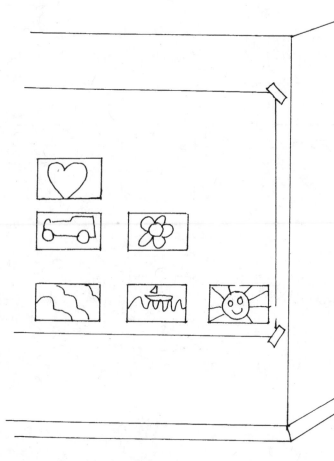

Artist's Favorite Paints

"What is your favorite color?" is an age-old familiar question. The answer becomes the basis of a colorful painting and graphing activity where artists use their favorite colors to create the graph.

Materials
✓ 9" x 12" white paper
✓ large sheet of butcher paper or craft paper (taped to the wall or chalkboard at child height)
✓ 1 favorite color of tempera paint for each artist
✓ paintbrushes of various sizes
✓ newspaper-covered work space
✓ masking tape
✓ black permanent marker

Process
1. Each artist chooses a favorite color of tempera paint and then paints with that color on the white paper. Any design or subject matter is fine, however, the painting is limited to one favorite color. Dry overnight.
2. When the painting is dry, draw, outline, write names, or make freeform designs on the painting with the permanent black marker.
3. Place loops of masking tape on the back corners of the paintings.
4. Take turns one at a time sticking the painting to the butcher paper on the wall. If one artist has the same favorite color as another artist, place their paintings next to each other.
5. After all the paintings are lined up, discuss which color seems to be the favorite of more artists, which colors are the least favorites. If all the single favorites are counted, are they more or less than the one favorite color?
   Note: Some children become very competitive in group graphing about which is best, who has the most, and so on. This is natural but can be softened so hurt feelings are minimized.

Variation
■ This same graph can be made in a smaller version by gluing squares or shapes of colored paper on a sheet of white paper. A single artist working independently could group favorite colors in order, from most favorite to least favorite.

More and Less Sculpture

   5+

B y comparing more and less, the young learner sees how quantities look and feel as a sculpture is built with wood scraps.

Materials

✓ wood scraps (rectangular and square block shapes work well)
✓ glue (or hot glue gun with adult assistance)
✓ flat board or plywood scrap for the base
✓ collage materials that are countable, such as
       cotton balls, corks, buttons, beads
✓ newspaper-covered work space

Process

1. Spread out the scraps of wood so they can be seen and handled easily. Explore the scraps, noting those that are long or short or in between.
2. Find a short piece and a long piece to use for the sculpture. Place them on the table. Move the rest of the scraps to the side.
3. Spread out the countable items on the table. Begin selecting some to use in the sculpture.
4. Glue as many countable items as possible to one side of the shorter wood scrap. Dry.
5. Glue as many countable items as possible to one side of the longer wood scrap. Let this piece dry too.
6. When both pieces are completely dry, decide which piece holds more and which one holds less.
7. Glue the pieces and their items to the flat base wood piece. Dry again.

Variations

■ Cover all sides of the short and long pieces with countable items.
■ Decorate with colored sand or tissue squares for a different effect.
■ Add to the base more short and long pieces that are different lengths with their counted items glued to them. These can also be put in order from shortest to longest, or from least to most.

5+ ⬤ ✋

graphing collage

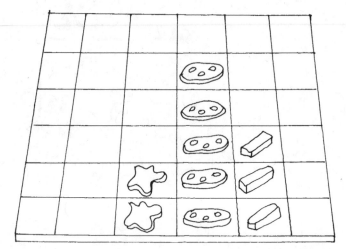

Cookie Graph

Graphing is a concept that can be explored and mastered by young children through creative art. It's one of those skills that incorporates a host of other math skills, namely: counting, comparing, sorting, and measuring. Creating a Cookie Graph requires two days to complete.

Materials

✓ yard stick and marker
✓ large sheet of craft paper or a piece of cardboard
✓ a variety of clay cookie sculptures (or use real cookies)
✓ collage items for decorating clay cookies (optional)
✓ white glue
✓ magazine pictures of cookies (optional)
✓ crayons (optional)

Process

1. With a yard stick and a marker, an adult draws squares on the paper or cardboard in a grid, measuring squares about 3" x 3". Fill the entire paper or cardboard with a grid of squares.
2. The artists create a wide and varied assortment of play-cookie sculptures for the project, possibly the day before. Decorate the clay cookies with collage items before baking or paint them after they cool.
3. Sort and group the cookies by similarities, differences, favorites, or invent other categories.
4. When the cookies have been sorted into groups, glue the first group on the paper, one per square, all in a line.
5. Glue the second group of clay cookies in a new line, one per square.
6. Glue the third group in another new line and so on. The lines will be of different lengths depending on how many cookies of each type there are (see illustration).
7. When all the cookie groups have been glued, look at the design. Which cookies have the most? Which have the least? Which has the longest line?
8. After the glue dries, paste pictures of real cookies in the blank squares or fill in the blank squares with bright colors of paper or paint. Although the result is a graph, the creative placement of the unique clay cookies will create pattern and design possibilities.

Exploring Number Value

Chain Graph

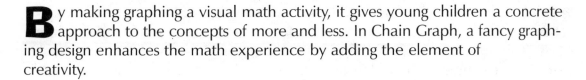

By making graphing a visual math activity, it gives young children a concrete approach to the concepts of more and less. In Chain Graph, a fancy graphing design enhances the math experience by adding the element of creativity.

Materials

✓ box filled with different colored paper strips for chains (all the same length)
✓ tape, white glue, stapler
✓ poster board or butcher paper for the base material
✓ tempera paints and brushes

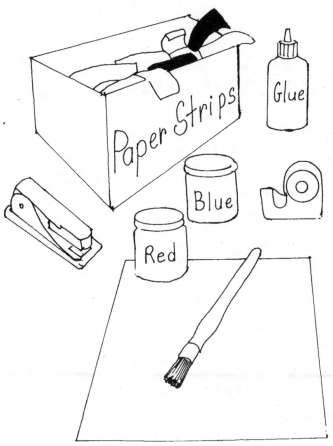

Process

1. The adult begins by filling a box with colored paper strips for making chains. Fill the box with no more than 20 of any one color and no more than 5 total colors. (Try to make sure that each color has a different number of strips. For instance: precount 5 red strips, 14 yellow strips, 1 blue strip, and 10 green strips. Or ask the artist and supply the colors and number of strips desired.)
2. The artist sorts through the box of paper strips and groups the strips by color on the table.
3. Make a chain for each color. Use tape, glue, or a stapler.
4. Then tape each single-colored chain as it is completed to the poster board at the topmost edge. The lengths of the chains will become readily visible as they hang down.
   Note: Chains can be sorted and put in order from shortest to longest before taping them to the poster board, but this is not required.
5. In the areas on the poster board that have no chains, apply paint to decorate the remainder of the graph. Dry.
6. Look at the Chain Graph and see which chains and colors have the most or least links, and which are the shortest and longest.

Variations

■ Use the same colored strips, but instead of chains, paste them on the poster board in a color grouped design that shows which colors have the most or least.
■ Make graphs from other precounted art materials, such as art tissue, cotton balls, leaves, pinecones, pebbles, stickers, or labels or any variety of collage items.

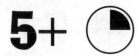

5+

time
drawing

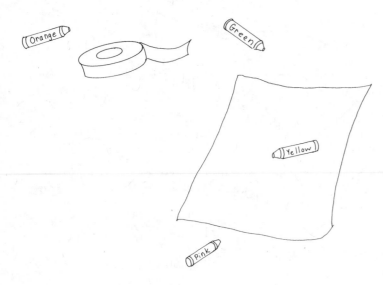

Ten Count Squiggles

When a child can count to any number (not necessarily to ten), counting can be a way to measure time. In Ten Count Squiggles, a friend or another person counts to ten while the young artist colors, draws, scribbles, and squiggles within the time frame of ten counts.

Materials
✓ crayons
✓ large sheets of drawing paper
✓ masking tape
✓ a friend to count

Process
1. Tape a sheet of large drawing paper to the table.
2. With a "Ready, Set, Go," the artist begins to scribble and squiggle with crayons as the counting friend counts to ten in a normal counting voice.
3. When the counter reaches ten he says, "Time's Up!" and the artist must stop squiggling.
4. Next, the counter and the artist trade places, if they choose, and the new artist has a turn to scribble and squiggle as the new counter counts to ten.

Variations
■ If the counter can't count to ten yet, counting to any number is fine, and counting over and over is fine too. For instance, the counter could count, "One, two, three; one, two, three; one, two, three" several times in a row.
■ If the artist doesn't want to stop coloring when time is up, more time for coloring can be worked out, or more counting can be added to the session. This activity should be fun!
■ Use the counting-time method for other art techniques such as painting, rolling clay shapes, building a sculpture, and so on.

My Drawing Portfolio

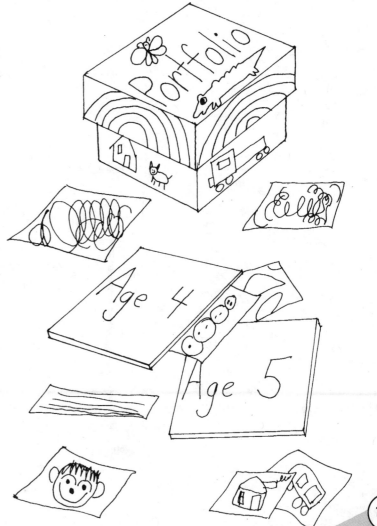

5+

When a child saves her artwork over a period of weeks, months, and years, she can see herself grow in artistic skill while keeping track of memories and experiences. The portfolio can be a box, a scrapbook, or a simple folder.

Materials

- ✓ cardboard box
- ✓ single cardboard sheets
- ✓ large stick-on labels
- ✓ artwork and drawings to fill the portfolio
- ✓ stickers (optional)
- ✓ colored pens
- ✓ white glue
- ✓ crayons

Process

The portfolio can be started at any age the child is ready to start saving artwork and drawings. A file box plain with handles or a cardboard box with a slip-on lid (such as reams of copier paper come in) work well.

1. Decorating the file box is optional with crayons, pens, or stickers. Glue on flat paper decorations or drawings, too. Set the box aside.
2. Spread out the drawings that are going into the portfolio.
3. Place a stick-on label onto the back of the drawing.
4. Write the age or date the drawing was made on the label. Let the young artists write the information if they can.
5. Put drawings in order from the youngest age to the oldest age.
6. Next, label cardboard sheets with ages to be used as dividers in the box. These can be decorated if desired.
7. Put the cardboard sheets in the box.
8. Place the drawings behind each sheet with the matching age.
9. As time goes by, add more drawings to the box. Look back and enjoy the progress, the memories and the works of art.

Variations

- Create a scrapbook portfolio and tape or glue the artwork on the pages.
- Photograph artwork and drawings. Save the photos in an album instead of the actual artwork.

171

5+ ◐ ✋ (caution)

**time
painting**

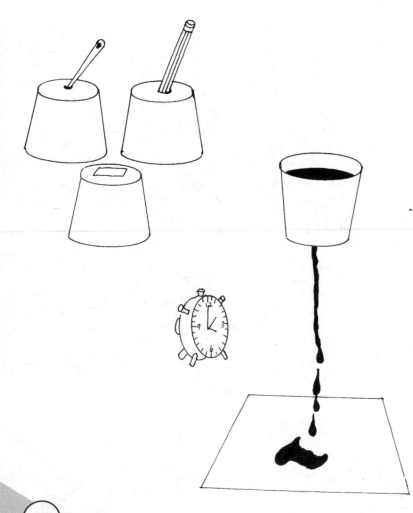

Speed Painting

When first exploring the concept of measuring time, young children can experiment with timing how long it takes for something to happen. In this experience, the young artist paints designs by letting paint drip through a hole in a paper cup.

Materials
✓ newspaper-covered work space
✓ masking tape
✓ tempera paints mixed thin in small milk cartons or containers
✓ paper cups
✓ poking tools with different sized points, such as
    darning needle, pencil, toothpick, bamboo skewer
✓ egg timer
✓ paper
✓ tray

Process
1. Cover the workspace with newspaper. Tape the newspaper to the table to prevent slipping.
2. Mix tempera paints to a thin consistency in the small milk cartons. Mix as many colors as desired.
3. Poke a hole in one of the paper cups with the darning needle (adult help may be needed for this step). Then poke a hole in another paper cup with a toothpick and another with a pencil point. Each hole should be a different size from every other hole.
4. Place a piece of masking tape over each hole on the outside of each paper cup.
5. Pour paint into each cup about half full. All the cups should have the same amount of paint, but they may have different colors.
6. Place the egg timer on the table, then a piece of paper for the design and one of the cups of paint.
7. Set the egg timer at 3 minutes to begin. Remove the piece of tape and let the paint drip and run from the hole, moving the cup about to create a design on the paper. When the timer rings say, "Time's Up!" and set the cup aside on the tray.
8. Visually note how much paint flowed and how much design was made.
9. Repeat this process with each cup and new sheets of paper for each design.
10. When complete, compare the designs made with large holes, small holes, and medium holes.

Exploring Number Value

Art Medium Index

Math Skills Index

Materials Index